7 STEPS TO

KNOWING, DOING AND

EXPERIENCING

THE WILL OF

GOD

FOR TEENS

TOM BLACKABY   MIKE BLACKABY   DANIEL BLACKABY

7 STEPS TO
KNOWING, DOING AND
EXPERIENCING
THE WILL OF
GOD

FOR TEENS

ILLUSTRATIONS
BY CORY JONES

EXPERIENCING
GOD
AT HOME

B&H
PUBLISHING GROUP
Nashville, Tennessee

ISBN: 978-1-4336-7983-4

Published by B&H Publishing Group
Nashville, Tennessee

Tom Blackaby is represented by the literary agency of
Wolgemuth & Associates, Inc.

Dewey Decimal Number: 248.83
Subject Heading: GOD—WILL \ CHRISTIAN LIFE \ TEENAGERS

1 2 3 4 5 6 7 8 9 • 18 17 16 15 14 13

DEDICATION

To my three great kids—Erin, Matt, and Conor—for giving me so many good stories to tell. I am proud of you all and privileged to be your dad.
—*Tom*

To my parents for everything. Also, to the amazing group of young adults I lead every week at First Baptist Church in Jonesboro, Georgia. You guys help me experience God every day as I see Him at work in each of your lives.
—*Mike*

To my loving parents for providing me the privilege of growing up in a home where walking with God was always something real, vibrant, and exciting.
—*Dan*

CONTENTS

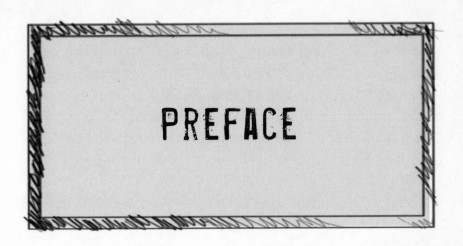

PREFACE

"GOD IS DEAD!"

That's what atheist German philosopher Friedrich
Nietzsche once claimed. He believed there was no room
for God in a modern society. If there were gods, they
were us. People have been making up their own gods
since time began, preferring a god of the imagination
over the God who created them. But to those who know
Him, God is not dead! We don't worship a God who is
absent or even distant.

God is alive, and He wants you to know it.
Not only that, He wants you to know Him.

Thousands of books exist about God; it would take a
lifetime to read them all. *Knowing God* by J. I. Packer is
an excellent one. Or, if you've never read the classic
about following God, *The Cost of Discipleship* by Dietrich
Bonhoeffer, that's one of the best there is. A more current read that's popular is *Not a Fan* by Kyle Idleman.
And of course, one of the best books ever written on
God is *Mere Christianity* by C. S. Lewis.

Books have been written about fearing God, loving God, obeying God, resisting God, even ignoring God and hating God. Many atheists have even published books about God! But that shouldn't surprise anyone, because God created us to be curious about Him. He gave us a soul that longs after Him. He wants us to experience Him.

Experiencing God goes deeper than knowing or following Him. Most non-Christians (and lots of believers too) consider the Christian faith to be a dusty list of rules and thou-shalt-nots, a yawn-fest of doctrines and unpronounceable theological terminology.[1]

But thankfully, millions of Christians know that's not true at all—because they have experienced God. They know Him personally. We hope you're included in that number. If not, you can be. That's what this book is all about.

Let's be honest. Most of us don't want to be observers of life; we want to experience it. Well, that's exactly what God wants for us. He doesn't just want us to read about Him and talk about Him; He designed us to experience Him.

NO, GOD IS NOT DEAD, NOR IS HE ABSENT.

God once encouraged His people, the scattered nation of Israel, with these words: *"For I know the plans I have for you . . . plans for your welfare, not for disaster, to give you a future and a hope"* (JEREMIAH 29:11). This same God has plans for each one of us as well.

---

1. "Would you care for some premillennial dispensationalism and a side of soteriological conceptualizations?"

This book is designed not only to help you discover those plans, but even more than that, we want you to come to know the One who holds your future. We wrote it to help you experience the joy of walking intimately with God.

There are three contributors to this book. We share a last name and a bloodline, but we've each walked a unique path as we've discovered God's plans for our life one day at a time. Since you are about to join us on the journey through the pages of this book, we should probably share a little about who we are:

Mike

I'm the oldest (and wisest) of three siblings, and at the time of this writing, I'm currently working toward my PhD in Apologetics and Worldview. That's a long-winded way of saying, "I'm forced to read a lot!" I currently live in Atlanta, Georgia, but I grew up in Canada, so living in the south has been somewhat of a culture (and climate) shock. I minister to a diverse group of amazing young adults, most of them in their late teens or early twenties. I love my job!

God clearly called me to the ministry when I was eighteen. Although it terrified me, I took that step forward and have never looked back. And what a journey! I wouldn't trade what I do for anything. Well, maybe one thing. . . .

I'm a musician who still holds a not-so-secret desire of becoming a rock star. (Any band out there looking for a drummer?) I also love hockey. Oh, and geeky fantasy/science-fiction stuff. You can follow my blog at mike blackaby.com.

Dan

I am the middle (and most handsome) of those three siblings and the perfect younger brother to Mike. I am finishing my Masters of Divinity degree just outside of San Francisco, California. In 2010 I married my amazing wife Sarah. My passion is using the creative arts (especially writing) for God's higher purposes. When God first called me into ministry, I was reluctant because I thought it meant giving up this passion. Instead, God has asked me to make it my ministry!

I've recently released my first fantasy/adventure novel *Legend of the Book Keeper*, the first book in a planned trilogy infused with spiritual themes and allegory.[2] I also love hockey (doesn't every Canadian?), baseball, and European heavy metal bands.

Tom

I am the second of five (yes, five) kids. My older brother is Mike and Dan's dad, which, if you do the math, makes me their favorite uncle. I've always enjoyed music. In fact, I currently own eleven different musical instruments. I played basketball and soccer in school and loved going to the gym to shoot baskets for hours. I married a girl I met in our youth group when my dad was a pastor in Canada. We have a daughter aged twenty, and two sons, nineteen and thirteen.

---

2. Check out danielblackaby.com for more details.

I've worked with young people for many years; now I love to see my own kids playing the same sports I grew up loving, playing drums and keyboard, laughing around the kitchen table, and growing in their own relationships with God.

I've traveled to more than forty countries so far in the ministry God has given me, and I never get tired of seeing new places where God is powerfully active. I'm thrilled to write this book with my two nephews. My contribution to the book is supposed to be the "seasoned veteran" perspective of a dad and world traveler. (In other words, I'm the "not cool" one! But I have my moments.)

In 1990, God led my father, Henry Blackaby, to write the Bible study *Experiencing God*. The publisher intended it to be a twelve-week study to be used within our denomination. No one, especially my dad, had any idea what an impact his work would have on Christians around the world. Multiple millions of copies have been sold worldwide. *Experiencing God* has been translated into more than fifty languages so far. People from numerous professions, backgrounds, and cultures have gone through the study—including prisoners on death row, soldiers stationed overseas, political leaders, business professionals, CEOs of Fortune 500 companies, artists, actors, musicians, and doctors. Members of both protestant and Catholic congregations have studied the *Seven Realities of Experiencing God* and applied them to their lives.

My dad (known as "Grandpa" to Mike and Dan) is a humble, reserved Canadian. But since he was a teenager, Henry experienced God's profound activity in and through his life. That's the way God often chooses to work. The Bible records story after story of God working mightily through ordinary men and women.

The three of us have been around the world, and there is not a place we go where someone doesn't say, "*Experiencing God* changed my life forever." And now we've been invited to put the study in a form specifically for young people.

You've probably heard the term Millennial Generation. If you are between the ages of twelve and thirty-two, you are considered a "millennial." You face both challenges and opportunities that your parents and grandparents could only dream of. Your generation has some momentous decisions to make about your personal life, about relationships, and about God.

As every graduating valedictorian will tell you, you are standing on the threshold of your future. If ever there were a time to "get it right," this is it. But you don't have to do it blindly.

God wants to guide you.

There is no shortage of advice out there. It's a daunting task to sift through the options and decide who is trying to sell you a load of goods and who's telling you the truth.

Only God has the corner on truth.

Like most young people, you probably wonder sometimes if anyone knows what you're going through, or if anyone even cares.[3]

---

3. This generation is the largest in history. Yet, it is also one of the most lonely and depressed.

> **God knows, and He cares deeply.**

In putting this book together, our joint desire is that whoever reads it will hear from God and enjoy walking with Him in a close, personal way. So get ready for an exciting journey, as we approach the seven principles that have transformed millions of lives and deliver them to you, just for you, in a way that you can apply to your life—starting today. Along the way, we know that you will discover some amazing biblical truths and come to experience God in a real and personal way.

THE BEGINNING: KNOWING AND DOING GOD'S WILL

"For I have come down from heaven, not to do My will, but the will of Him who sent Me."—JESUS (JOHN 6:38)

MY DIGNITY FOR AN AUTOGRAPH

I (Mike) spent my first year in college working at a local coffee/sandwich shop. I liked it, but it was not the place you'd expect celebrities to frequent. So when the coach of the local NHL hockey team walked in one day, everyone got a little excited. And I was the worst. . . .

"Look! It's Darryl Sutter!" I squealed, giddily running back and forth behind the counter, desperate to serve him. When an order for chili appeared on the screen, I exploded into a flurry of activity, packing up his meal in record time. I arranged it "just so" in a take-out bag and tossed in a couple extra packets of crackers. After all, this guy was not only an NHL coach, he was a member of the famed Sutter family: seven brothers and they all played or coached in the National Hockey League.

He approached the counter.

He opened his mouth to speak.

Oh sweet mercy, I thought, *he's going to say something to me!*

"I'm sorry; I actually ordered that to dine in."

I snatched the bag off the counter, stuttering my apologies, and spilled chili everywhere in my attempt to correct the mistake. He suppressed a smile and thanked me, finding a table in the far corner to eat.

When he finished his meal, he got up to leave. That was my cue. I mustered every ounce of courage and blurted, "Mr. Sutter sir, c-could I g-get your a-autograph p-please?" I hastily thrust a take-out bag in his face.

"Sure, do you have a pen?"

Panic tugged at my stomach. My eyes darted around the room. Sweat poured from my brow. I sheepishly excused myself to the kitchen.

"EVERYBODY STOP!" I hollered. "FOR THE LOVE OF ALL YOU HOLD SACRED, I NEED A PEN!" Thankfully I got my pen, and I got my autograph, but that was the last time Sutter darkened our doors.

IT'S PERSONAL

Many people view God the way Mike saw that hockey coach. They admire Him—but from a distance. They are in awe of Him and may even venture to ask for something now and then. But when it comes down to it, they have no real relationship with Him. They don't know God, and they think He doesn't know them.

However, the Bible portrays a God who not only knows you, but wants to be known by you. In fact, He wants every person from every nation around the globe to know Him (1 Timothy 2:4).

God is commonly perceived as a cosmic version of the (spoiler alert!) mythical Santa Claus, always watching us and assessing our behavior so He can determine the size of our annual payout. Or to use a less creepy metaphor, others think of Him the way you might view a majestic animal like, say, a lion in a zoo—intriguing to study but safely separated from us. Still others treat Him as simply an intellectual concept or idea that may be interesting to think and talk about, but doesn't have much of an impact on how we live.

The Bible reveals that God is not merely an outside observer of our lives,

A movement in the 1800s called "Deism" basically claimed that God created the world, but then left it to run according to its own natural laws. He never intervened, so that meant no miracles and no personal relationship with His creation. One of America's most famous Deists was Thomas Jefferson. He believed that God set the natural laws in place, wound the world up like a clock, and then stepped back to let things run their course. In fact, he was so adamant that God did not intervene in nature that he cut out of his New Testament every passage that recorded a miracle!

and He's not a mighty-but-confined being who exists for our pleasure, whom we can admire whenever it suits us. Nor is He a high concept that can only be discussed by boring theology professors.

Pause for a minute to think about the way you perceive God. How would you describe Him in a sentence or two? Now, go a step deeper and consider how the way you live expresses what you think He is like. We're not presupposing that every reader equates God to a super-sized St. Nick or merely an object of curiosity, but we do assume that if you're reading this book you want to know Him more fully than you do now. So first, we hope to heighten your awareness of two things:

JOHN STUART MILL

It is important that we understand and accept who God really is, rather than try to create Him into what we want Him to be. This was something that philosopher John Stuart Mill just could not accept. He said, "Whatever power such a being may have over me, there is one thing which he shall not do: he shall not compel me to worship him. I will call no being good, who is not what I mean when I apply that epithet to my fellow creatures; and if such a being can sentence me to hell for not so calling him, to hell I will go."

 1. God has a will for your life.

 2. He wants to reveal it to you personally.

The first prerequisite for knowing God's will is to know God Himself. It's one thing to admire God from afar, but walking according to His will goes considerably deeper than that.

WHO IS GOD?

This is a huge question. The Bible introduces us to the God who created the entire universe. Not only did God bring everything into being, but at the grand climax of creation He created humanity in His own image, endowing us with the capability of reflecting His characteristics by the way we live.[4] This is extremely important, because God didn't need to create anything. The fact that He chose to create the world and place us in it tells us He must have a purpose for doing so. Further, the fact that He created us in His image lets us know that God has a unique plan for humans. Our likeness to God sets us apart from the rest of creation. Only human beings have the capacity to relate to God in a personal way.[5] In fact, that's why He designed us in the first place.

The book of Genesis (chapter 3) describes what happened to spoil the party: the first humans, whom the Bible names as Adam and Eve, used the gift of free will to rebel against God. Humanity has been following their example ever since. That's the bottom line of what sin is—rebellion against holy God—and that's what separates us from Him.

Here's the good news: The rest of Scripture is the account of how God has been actively working in the

---

4. There is a joke about some arrogant scientists who mock God by claiming they, too, can make human beings out of the dust like God did in Genesis. God says, "Okay, I challenge you to a contest where we will each attempt to make humans out of the dirt." The scientists start working when God stops them, "Hey, get your own dirt!" *Oh snap!*

5. You're not likely to see a rock pouring its heart and soul out to God in a personal relationship!

WHY FREE WILL?

You may ask yourself, "Why would God bother to create us with free will if it opens up the possibility that we could deeply hurt Him? Think of it this way. The iPhone has an incredible app called "Siri," which is basically a computer in your phone that can respond to your every command. It never disobeys. But what kind of relationship can you have with a phone? Consider a dog. It is a little more complicated than a phone, and it will love you back unconditionally. But what's the deepest relationship you could ever have with a dog? Finally, consider your best friend (perhaps a childhood friend, your boyfriend/girl-friend, a sibling, or a parent). This person, because of free will, has the ability to hurt you more deeply than a phone or a dog. But who would trade in one for the other? The fact is, love is not really love if it is forced. We, as humans, have the ability to hurt God deeply, but we also have the unique ability to know and love Him as nothing else in creation ever could.

world to restore the relationship that was lost in the Garden of Eden, so we can walk closely with Him and know what's on His heart.

If you've picked up this book to read, chances are you're interested in knowing and doing God's will.[6] Just as God has a will and purpose for this world, He also has one for your life. And the best news is, He wants you to know all about it.

IF AT FIRST YOU DON'T SUCCEED . . . MAYBE YOU SHOULDN'T DRIVE

 The piercing squeal of burning tires roared over the sound of the rambunctious crowd. An entire lifetime boiled down to this. Swerving my car around the final turn, I (Dan) gazed toward the finish line. *This is who I am; I was born to drive. . . .* Punching the car into fifth, I made cruel mockery of my fellow racers. Almost there! Then I . . . *heard a voice?*

"Time to go!" the voice called.

I turned my Xbox off. "Coming, Dad!" It was the big day.

March 7: I had finally reached the wise age of fourteen, thus making me eligible to receive my learner's driving permit. The only thing blocking my path toward

---

6. If you were given this book as a "white elephant" gift, we're sorry, but please give it a shot anyway!

racing greatness was a measly twelve-question exam. *Not a problem.*

Suddenly I remembered that the registrar's office had mailed me a study guide three months prior. I dug it out from under my bed, blew off the dust, and removed the shrink wrap. *Study?* I chuckled and tossed it back to the floor. *Naahh, they don't call me Daniel "Dale Earnhardt Jr." Blackaby for nothing! I've seen Dad drive—how hard can it be?*

March 9: Bursting through the doors, I strutted into the testing center oozing confidence out of every pore. "Let's get this baby over with and hit the road! Woo!" Working my magic I finished in record time.

Results: What?! I failed? This can't be! I demand a recount! Fine, I'll just get it tomorrow.

March 10: More determined and still suspecting a miscount, I marched into the building. "Lay it on me. I've got a date with the open road in thirty minutes!"

Results: Those trick questions get you every time.

March 11: I cautiously poked my head through the doorway, slightly stuttering as I asked for my test. "Come on in, Dan! We've been expecting you." (Did I detect a note of mockery in that cheery greeting?)

Results: Isn't the third time supposed to be a charm?

March 12: My limping body forced its way through the doors, head hung low and a twitch in my left eye. "Do you guys accept bribes?"

Results: Wow, could have sworn those last nine questions were right. . . . Walking was good enough for Jesus, wasn't it?

March 13: Crawling on all fours, I inched my feeble body toward the counter. I had a final ace up my sleeve: groveling. "Have mercy on me! Don't make me do that horrible test again!"

Results: "Daniel: you passed. Barely." Proof that God still does miracles!

I sauntered out to the parking lot, where my long-suffering dad was waiting. Shooing him out of the driver's seat *(What? Did he have no confidence that I would pass?)*, I got in and snapped on my seat belt with a decisive *click*. After adjusting the rearview mirror, I only had one question for dad.

"Okay, which one is the gas pedal?"

MAYBE IT AIN'T BROKE AFTER ALL?

Assumptions can be costly. The truth is, as hard as we may try to live according to our own best thinking, we aren't as "in control" of our destiny as we might think. In fact, we often don't know nearly as much as we think we do!

One rainy day, I (Mike) was getting drenched as I trudged across my college campus. Growing increasingly aggravated with a broken umbrella, I was forced to keep one arm extended, pushing the top up just to keep it open. Eventually I made it to class. But I was wet, sore, and angry. I vented my frustration to a classmate. She said nothing but reached over and pressed a small button on the handle. The umbrella immediately shot into its usable position, flinging water drops over everyone in the class. Who knew?[7]

PLAN A

Most people can figure out the elementary mechanics of simple things like umbrellas, but isn't it true that many of us stumble through life trying to manage by our own wits? We don't even investigate, so we miss out on how life is supposed to work at its best. We nod our heads when someone tells us, "God has a plan for your life!" While in our hearts we think, "That's great, but I'm gonna make a Plan B just in case!" But why not go with

---

7. That awkward moment when you suddenly realize you're a moron.

Plan A—God's plan? Why settle for anything less than God's best for you? God intends for us to experience so much more through Him than we could ever do on our own. Sadly, many people choose to live their lives according to their own sub-par Plan B, and they end up missing out on all that God had for them.

Many people would have us believe there is no Plan A, or any plan at all. They say the only way to survive is by our own ingenuity and instincts.[8] The Bible emphatically says otherwise. God has not left us to navigate through life on our own. If that were the case, He would not have given us the Scriptures, let alone sent His Son to die in our place on a cross!

It comes down to a choice. Are we going to live according to our best or God's best? The outcome is determined by who we listen to and whose will we choose to follow.

GOD'S WILL OR YOURS?

If you're in high school right now, here's something to consider: What part has the Great Commission played in your post-graduation planning? If you're not familiar with the term, the Great Commission is how Christians commonly refer to the final instructions Jesus gave just before His ascension to heaven. Jesus told His disciples,

"All authority has been given to Me in heaven and on earth. Go, therefore, and make disciples of all nations, baptizing them in the name of the Father and of the Son and of the Holy Spirit, teaching them to observe everything I have commanded you. And remember, I am with you always, to the end of the age" (MATTHEW 28:18–20).

---

8. Considering that Dan still reads the instructions on how to make instant cup of soup, this is not a good thing.

That's a big assignment to leave with His disciples and those who watched Him ascend to heaven. Had that assignment been meant only for those standing there, the good news about Christ's sacrifice for us would have long since disappeared with those people when they died. But fortunately each generation has taken up the mission to reach its own generation for Christ.

Is there ever a better time in life to take that commandment seriously than at graduation time? That's when people set in motion the plans that will determine their career and much of their future. Yet many young Christians plan for college or a vocation in the very same way as those who aren't followers of Christ. They neglect to consider the plans God may have for their lives.

Even Christian parents are guilty of guiding their graduating sons and daughters according to finances, their own alma mater, or whatever will keep them close to home (or in some cases, send them far away!).

C. T. STUDD

C. T. Studd had the kind of life anyone would dream of. He was an exceptionally gifted cricket player, he was a Cambridge grad, and he inherited a ton of money when his father passed away.

However, he gave up his life of comfort to be a missionary in China and in Africa. What would compel a man to give up everything in order to share the good news of Jesus around the world? He took the Great Commission seriously. It wasn't about his will but God's will.

One of Studd's most famous statements was: "Some want to live within the sound of a church or chapel bell; I want to run a rescue shop within a yard of hell."

That can be a costly oversight. We're not saying you shouldn't ask yourself the usual questions:

"What am I good at?"

"What is my passion?"

"What's the best geographical choice for me?"

"Should I take a year off to earn some money or travel?"

(Here's a biggie.) "What school do I have a scholarship for?"

But the non-Christian senior asks the same questions without any direction from God. What's the difference? The difference is following your own agenda versus seeking God's plan for you.

If you want to know and do the will of God, it starts by focusing on His will, not yours. It means having a "God-centered" view of life. Now is the best time to acquire that view.

Perhaps you already have a sense of what God wants you to do, maybe not specifically, but enough to know what your next step should be. When Mike was eighteen years old, he had a clear word from God about going into the ministry.[9] Daniel took a gap year after graduating to do some traveling and mission work, and it was during that time his own calling was clarified. Tom's story is completely different from both of these. No two people have the exact same story. God doesn't always choose to let us in on specific details up front. He wants us to follow Him, not a blueprint.

The point is, when we seek God's will, we have to do what He tells us, and that first step can be the scariest.

---

9. Check out his testimony in *When Worlds Collide: Stepping Up and Standing Out in an Anti-God Culture.*

Perhaps God's specific will for your life is not very clear to you right now. Don't panic. Hopefully by the end of this book you will have a better idea of what that looks like.

But another consideration is that maybe God has given you direction, but you're choosing not to do what He's said. Most long distance runners will tell you that the hardest part of their training was lacing up their running shoes on day one. In other words, committing to get the thing done can often be the most difficult. Surely it's no accident that the apostle Paul used the metaphor of running a race when he taught about living out the Christian life. You can't finish a race you don't start.[10]

Many of us want to know up front what we're getting ourselves into when we say yes to God. But He simply asks us to take the first step, and then the second and so on. Take it from us, this journey will be rewarding.

HAND OVER THE DRILL BIT, NOW!

I (Tom) thought I could save a lot of money by doing the project myself (Mistake #1). It seemed straightforward enough: drill a hole through the first floor into the basement, run the internet cable through, and connect to the computer. Voila! Internet connection!

I went to the hardware store, bought

---

10. Well, except when Dan went running and later found himself amidst hundreds of other runners wearing pink shirts. He had accidentally joined a run for breast cancer awareness!

the longest drill bit I could find, and prepared for surgical maneuvers. I put on my wife's rubber dish-gloves, so I would not have a shocking experience if a stray electrical wire happened to be nearby.

Straight through the floor, right near the wall, easy does it. And yes, we're through. We were through all right. Checking downstairs, I saw my drill bit poking through the middle of the hallway ceiling. NOT what I had intended, but we can improvise.

Next was to drill through the hallway wall and into the office. It gave me a little bit of trouble, but when I looked through the hole, I could see the light clearly from the next room. Soon the cable was threaded through the holes, along the wall and inserted into the computer with great success. The only trouble was the presence of a foul and persisting odor. I thought perhaps someone had spread manure in a nearby garden. The strange thing was the smell came from *inside* the house, not from the outside.

I asked a friend to check on my sewer back-up valve, and it turned out to be fine. Next he looked at my neat little hole in the wall. He took out a carpenter's knife and cut a box around the hole. He peeled back the wall and sighed knowingly (we'd been friends for awhile).

I had drilled right through the middle of a sewer pipe coming from the top floor. Now I know a lot of garbage goes over the Internet, but this was ridiculous.

With a stern look, my friend said, "Hand over the drill bit, now."

Many times, doing it yourself can lead you into trouble. Because God designed life and because God designed us, He knows so much better than we do how to live it. Just as it is foolish to try and do something alone that you know you're not qualified to do, we often insist on living life according to our own best ability. When we do this, the results often stink.

> "We never keep to the present. We recall the past; we anticipate the future as if we found it too slow in coming and were trying to hurry it up, or we recall the past as if to stay it's too rapid flight . . . We almost never think of the present, and if we do think of it, it is only to see what light it throws on our plans for the future . . . Thus we never actually live, but hope to live, and since we are always planning how to be happy, it is inevitable that we should never be so."
>
> —BLAISE PASCAL [PENSEES]

Many of us see God as a kind of genie who exists to make our dreams come true. Just listen to the prayers we pray:

✓ Please God help me pass this class.

✓ Please help me to get this job.

✓ Please provide me with a girlfriend/boyfriend.

✓ Please make me feel better.

✓ Please give me more friends.

✓ Please use Your mighty power to keep Dad from finding out I scratched his car.

Rarely, it seems, do we stop and ask, "God, what do You want me to do?"

Are we even prepared for what His answer might be? Are you ready to follow God's will, even if it involves trials? Jesus modeled this for us while He was moments away from facing the horror of the cross. He prayed, "Father, if You are willing, take this cup away from Me— nevertheless, not My will, but Yours, be done" (Luke 22:42). Before we ever ask God to reveal His will, we should first ask ourselves if we are ready to obey it.

WHOSE WILL ARE YOU SEEKING?

We're hoping we've not scared you away from seeking God's will. That's not our intention, but we do want to present a realistic and biblical understanding of what this all means. When Jesus said, "For I have come down from heaven, not to do My will, but the will of Him who sent Me" (John 6:38), He knew it would ultimately lead Him to die on a cross. God's plans for us are part of a bigger purpose than just our own personal comfort. Our wildest dreams for our lives are usually not God's dreams[11] (Isaiah 55:9; Ephesians 3:20).

In fact, it seems that more and more people today are struggling with boredom, of all things! How can a Christian ever be bored?[12] The problem is not that there

---

11. When Mike was little, he wanted more than anything to be a cowboy when he grew up (probably due to being born in Texas). However, one day a distraught Mike came home and brought his concerns to his mom. He said, "Mom, nobody at church wants to be a cowboy. Nobody at school wants to be a cowboy. None of my friends want to be cowboys." On the verge of tears, he cried, "Those Indians are going to *kill* me!"

12. We are, of course, making a notable exception for math class.

is nothing to do; the problem is that many Christians are intent on living according to their own will instead of God's. When you follow God's will, we promise you that boredom will not show up in your vocabulary. There are so many things God desires to show us if we would only take the time to seek Him.

Often, when we ask God what His will is, we are really asking Him to bless our will. Our focus is "me-centered" instead of "God-centered." You never read in the Bible an instance of God coming to a person and saying "What would you like me to do? What do you think is best?" Yet when we pray, we often spend most of the time talking to God like we are the experts.

Daniel and his wife Sarah recently had the opportunity to meet a famous marriage expert, Gary Chapman.[13] As they waited, the people in front of them spent several long-winded minutes telling Gary all about their opinions on marriage! When Dan and Sarah stepped up, they had several questions ready for him. They walked away with some valuable counsel that they would not have received had they monopolized the conversation.

When you meet with God in prayer, make it a point to seek His will instead of just laying out your own plans. Remember that Jesus is Lord; He is the expert and you are not.[14]

We have some exciting things to share with you, but first we want to nail down what God's will looks like in its true perspective. Although it may not be easy or comfortable all the time, it is best. In fact, it's better than anything we could ever come up with on our own. Think

13. He is the author of *The Five Love Languages*, which has sold more than 5 million copies.
14. The word *Lord* generally refers to one who has power or authority.

about it, the God of the universe has a plan—and He wants you to be a part of it. History is full of examples of ordinary people that God used to do extraordinary things. The Bible overflows with stories of teenagers through whom God changed the world. That could be you, if you're willing to be obedient to God's will. If you're ready to follow Christ wherever He leads, then buckle up and get ready for the journey of a lifetime!

Here's a quick glimpse of what's ahead in the coming chapters. We'll be the first to acknowledge that there are usually no easy, universal "7 Steps" to anything worthwhile[15] because people are all different. These seven points do not combine into a magic formula that will turn you into the next Francis Chan. They are simply truths taken from the Bible and applied to your life. In Henry Blackaby's book, *Experiencing God*, he called them seven realities. We've chosen the term *steps* because each one takes you a little farther on your journey as you develop your own personal relationship with God. So here they are up front, and we'll look a little more closely at them in the chapters to come:

---

15. Well, except maybe baking cookies.

STEP 1

God is always at work around you.

STEP 2

God pursues a continuing love relationship with you that is real and personal.

STEP 3

God invites you to become involved with Him in His work.

STEP 4

God speaks by the Holy Spirit through the Bible, prayer, circumstances, and the church to reveal Himself, His purposes, and His ways.

STEP 5

God's invitation for you to work with Him always leads you to a crisis of belief that requires faith and action.

STEP 6

You must make major adjustments in your life to join God in what He is doing.

STEP 7

You come to know God by experience as you obey Him, and He accomplishes His work through you.

WALKING WITH GOD

1. Based on what you've read, how would you describe "God's will" to somebody?

2. How involved do you think God is in this world? In what ways have you seen God's activity?

3. Where have you seen God working in your own life?

4. What would you say "God's will" means in your life right now?

5. Have you been guilty of seeking your own plans over God's plans? If so, how can you begin to shift your focus from me-centered to God-centered?

1

GOD IS ALWAYS AT WORK AROUND YOU

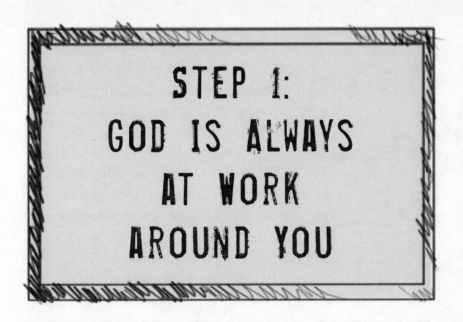

STEP 1: GOD IS ALWAYS AT WORK AROUND YOU

"Then Elisha prayed, 'Lord, please open his eyes and let him see.' So the Lord opened the servant's eyes. He looked and saw that the mountain was covered with horses and chariots of fire all around Elisha."
—2 KINGS 6:17

IT HELPS TO KNOW WHAT YOU'RE DOING

Charles Steinmetz was a brilliant mathematician and electrical engineer. After he retired from a long career at General Electric, a system breakdown had GE engineers stumped. Henry Ford called on Steinmetz as a consultant. Steinmetz refused any assistance, asking only for a notepad, a pencil, and a cot. For two days he listened to the machinery and scribbled on his notepad. Finally, he marked an X on the defective part with a piece of chalk

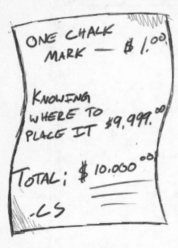

and billed GE for $10,000. The company was taken aback by his fee and protested, asking for an itemized bill. Steinmetz's reply read as follows: Making one chalk mark—$1.00.

Knowing where to place it—$9,999.00." They paid the bill!

Knowing what you're doing makes all the difference. Would you agree that God is wiser than we are? So if God has a purpose for our lives, and He has perfect knowledge of how best to fulfill that purpose, it becomes extremely important that we understand what He has in mind to do. Problems arise when we try to figure things out on our own.

In the previous chapter we talked about how God is involved in His creation. This chapter will begin to show how He is involved in your life, in particular. We're going to take the first step in helping you find God's will for your life.

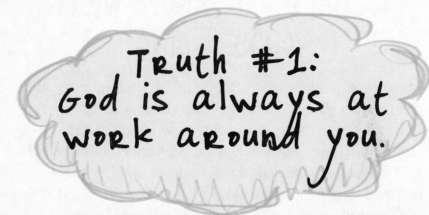

Truth #1: God is always at work around you.

Have you ever thought about that? Maybe it's a new concept to you. We've met many people who don't think this way. Unless they see something like, say, the milk in their cereal dividing a la Red Sea, they think they need to ask God to work. That's why you often hear people asking God to bless their plans when they pray before a church service or a mission project or a test or a job interview. Without meaning to, they're treating prayer like a coin that activates one of those claw machines that they can wield to get the desired prize.

Maybe you've heard the story of the man who got trapped on his roof during a flood. In the midst of the torrent, he cried out and asked God to save him from drowning. While he was still praying, a man in a boat came by and offered to help him. "That's okay," replied the man, "God will save me!" Then came a bigger boat and finally a rescue helicopter, but the man refused their help. He eventually drowned and went to

SIGNS

In this 2002 film, the world is visited by aliens. The story centers around a small family at their farm. Mel Gibson plays a nonpracticing priest, who has turned his back on God after a personal tragedy. However, the alien invasion forces him to rethink the way he sees the world. In a conversation with his brother, he says, "People break down into two groups. When they experience something lucky, group number one sees it as more than luck, more than coincidence. They see it as a sign, evidence, that there is someone up there, watching out for them. Group number two sees it as just pure luck. Just a happy turn of chance. . . . See what you have to ask yourself is, what kind of person are you? Are you the kind that sees signs, that sees miracles? Or do you believe that people just get lucky?"

heaven, where he asked God, "Why didn't you save me from drowning?" God replied, "I sent two boats and a helicopter!"

The way we pray reflects what we really believe about God. Too often, we act as though God won't do anything in the world until we ask Him. We're all guilty of this at times. Perhaps you've heard a worship leader pray and ask that God would "show up" in the service. But Jesus has already promised, "For where two or three are gathered together in My name, I am there among them" (Matthew 18:20).

There are three obstacles that can keep us from recognizing God's activity:

1) We don't look for it.

2) We're too distracted.

3) We mistake it for something else.

Let's look at these three issues more closely and take a lesson from each one of them.

Lesson #1: If you want to see God at work around you, be intentional to look for it.

A FRIENDLY REMINDER FROM SOME BARBED WIRE

I (Mike) used to like Capture the Flag. I was once under the impression that it was a safe and fulfilling way of releasing the aggressive manliness built into every male. I don't believe that anymore. Several years ago I attended a youth retreat where we decided to kick off the first night with a game of Capture the Flag. Excitement spread throughout the group as we waited for dark. We gathered in the main lodge for "debriefing," and our youth leader explained the rules to us, but I was so excited, I couldn't listen. I missed the last and most important piece of advice he gave. "And don't get too close to the boundaries," he said, "because there is a barbed wire fence on one side that may be hard to see in the dark. Have fun everyone."

All I heard was, "ahlkja hsbak ljsgkj sjhiua HAVE FUN EVERYONE!" I jumped up and raced outside.

The whistle blew, and I immediately dashed to the far side of the field where the tree cover was. It was completely dark now, and I knew I would stand a better chance of not being seen if I stuck to the edge. However, the other team had predicted my clever plan and had posted guards to wait. Before I could make it to safety, one of them spotted me. I started running as fast as I could to break their line of defense. My escape took me closer and closer to the edge until–CRASH!

My world turned upside down, and I felt a sharp pain in my legs, followed by a cold breeze, and then I was lying in the bushes. I had found the barbed wire! As I dragged myself to my feet, I realized I had no pants; the fence had completely torn them off! Blood was pouring down my leg. A couple of my friends helped me back to the lodge— a difficult task since they were laughing so hard they could barely hold themselves up. I spent the remainder of the game being nursed by our youth leader's wife.

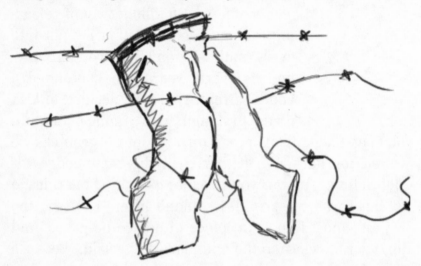

WHAT ARE YOU LOOKING FOR?

You usually don't see what you're not looking for. And sometimes, that can be very costly! You see, the issue is not God's presence; the problem is whether we'll recognize Him in our midst or not. Maybe God would say "I am here with you! But you guys are so concerned about your own agenda that you are missing Me." What a tragedy to show up at church week after week asking God to join us there, when He has been there all along waiting for us to recognize and obey Him.

It's easy to jump right into our prayer requests without even asking what God might want in the situation.

Jesus said, "But *seek first* the kingdom of God and His righteousness, and all these things will be provided for you" (Matthew 6:33, emphasis ours). What are you seeking first? Many of us put the things we want in front of seeking the kingdom. Then we fail to see God already at work around us, because we're looking around for what we want, not what He wants. You see what you are looking for.

RECOGNIZING GOD AT WORK

Recently, I (Mike) learned a lesson about identifying God at work. I had just led a group of young people on a mission trip to Orlando where we had ministered to the homeless.[16] When we got back, Justin, a fellow team member, asked me, "So what do you think God wants us to do here now that we're back?" We both agreed to pray and watch for God's activity.

The next day was Sunday, and while I was preparing to teach our Bible study class, in walked a stranger, about my age. By the end of the class, he'd shared some of his story with us. He had moved from California to get away from the gang lifestyle. Ten out of his twelve close friends were now dead, and the other two were in jail. He opened up to us and said, "I'm looking for a place to belong, because I need to get away from my old life."

On Monday I was at my office, which is housed in our church's Recreation Outreach Center. In came another

---

16. Check it out at straightstorlando.com.

guy I'd never seen before. He said he wanted to talk to a pastor about getting involved with church, since he knew his life needed to change. He had also recently moved to the area, and he, too, had come from a rough background. God obviously wanted to continue His work now that we had come back home. I honestly believe this was God's way of testing us. The Bible says that if you are faithful with a few things, God will trust you with more (Matthew 25:21). We had been obedient in Orlando, but would we continue to be obedient when we got back home?

Although these situations may seem obvious, it's surprising how easy it is to look right past the evidence of God's actions and miss it. God brought to my mind Romans 3:10–11: "There is no one righteous, not even one. There is no one who understands; there is no one who seeks God." Jesus said that nobody seeks after the Father unless God Himself draws them (John 6:44). This means that those who come asking about God and seeking Him are not doing that all on their own; God is at work in their lives. Because we were looking for it, Justin and I saw God's activity in both of these young men, and were able to respond appropriately.

There are opportunities all around us to see God at work, but if we don't take the time to stop and pray and seek God's heart, we will miss them every time. Mike and Dan's youth pastor growing up had a simple saying that he loved. He'd blurt out, "That's God!" every time he saw God at work. What a great reminder to be seeking the activity of God around us.

Lesson #2: If you want to see God's activity, cut back on the distractions.

Let's be honest, we live in a busy culture. With our phones glued to our hands, our eyes perpetually on a TV or computer screen, our iPods pulsating in our ears, and a million other diversions. It's no wonder we have a hard time hearing from God or seeing His will.

When was the last time you were quiet before God in prayer?[17]

We know it's not easy. All three of us are immersed in the same technology-and-entertainment-saturated culture as you, and it's tough to slow down and concentrate long enough to get in line with what God wants for our lives. The problem is, not only do we miss out when we don't acknowledge God's activity, it often costs us dearly.

SAINT FRANCIS OF ASSISI [1181–1226]

Francis grew up with many distractions. He came from a wealthy home and lived life frivolously with his friends, with no concern for anything beyond himself. Then God got a hold of his life. When he realized all that Jesus had done for him, he gave up everything (even the clothes off his back) to live in poverty and serve Christ through serving others. He became the founder of the Franciscan monks, and they are still active today. God may not be calling you to live in poverty, but are you willing to cleanse your life of distractions so that you are able to follow Him with your whole heart?

---

17. Maybe you thought you were a super-spiritual prayer warrior because whenever you spent time in prayer, God gave you visions. And then you realized you just kept falling asleep . . .

Lesson #3: If you want to recognize God at work, consider your situation from a new perspective.

KNOWING WHAT TO LOOK FOR

Perhaps our false expectations throw us off, and that's why we fail to see what God is doing right where we are. The Jewish people were looking for their Messiah to come crashing to earth like Thor, swinging his hammer to crush the Romans and free God's people from their oppressors. Not many expected their deliverer to come as a humble baby, born in a stable. But God doesn't work according to our expectations.

Our culture has conditioned us to equate comfort with blessing. Especially in North America, we falsely assume that if we are in discomfort, let alone in pain, God has abandoned us. That's not what the Bible teaches.

GOD AT WORK WHILE WE'RE HURTING

Did you know that God can work through the most painful moments in your life? It's sometimes hardest to see God when we're hurting. Maybe that's because we often turn our eyes inward when we suffer. But when we focus only on ourselves, it becomes more difficult to recognize that God works in these moments too.

DESTINED TO BE DISTRACTED?

Recent stats track the rise in media usage among young people. Did you know that around 75% of teens in America own cell phones today? Smartphones provide access to calling, texting, Internet, and MP3s. Also, 79% of teens own an iPod or MP3 player, and 80% own a gaming console. Of teens that are online, 73% use a social networking website. Statistics go out of date pretty fast, but the trend has been to see an increase in all of these areas. What does this tell us? That there are a lot of distractions out there waiting to steal our time if we let them. (Stats from pewinternet.org.)

Please don't misunderstand the point here. We're not dismissing pain lightly. Some of you may have endured unimaginable experiences. Or perhaps you are going through turmoil right now. It could be that you're just trying to "get through," and you think God has abandoned you. Not true![18]

What we want you to understand is this: God sees your pain. He knows about suffering. And sometimes you will see God most clearly through your tears.

SLEEPLESS NIGHTS

When I (Dan) was a young teenager, I developed severe insomnia. For the next several years it continued to get worse. It reached the point where I would be awake until five or six in the morning and could experience three or four nights in a row without a single minute of sleep. I was discouraged and confused. I was active in the leadership in my youth group, played on the worship team, and I was doing everything I thought I should as a Christian. So why was God allowing me to struggle?

God revealed His purposes to me at summer youth camp. It was the second night and our group had gathered to pray and share God's activity in our lives. I asked them to pray about my insomnia.[19] As I finished,

---

18. If you are experiencing a season of pain right now, we encourage you not to walk that road alone. That is why God places us within a church family. Take some time to call your pastor, talk to a parent, or seek out an adult in your church that you respect, and talk to them about the issues you are facing.
19. For a more detailed account of Dan's testimony check out Mike and Dan's book *When Worlds Collide: Stepping Up and Standing Out in an Anti-God Culture.*

a girl raised her hand. She shared with the group that she had been suffering from depression. One late night she had decided to commit suicide but had seen on her computer that I was logged on to MSN's instant messenger.[20] After venting, we had met together and talked through the night. She concluded by sharing, "Had Daniel not been awake to respond to that message, I would be dead today."

Then a boy spoke up. He had reached the end of his rope earlier that summer as well. One night, he had strapped ice packs to his wrists and was just waiting for them to go numb so he could cut them and end his life. As he waited, he decided that at least one person needed to know why he did it. It was four in the morning, but he had thought of me and how I was always up late. He called, and I answered the first ring. He confessed, "If Daniel had not answered that phone call—I would be dead today too."

I watched in awe as a domino effect happened and other teenagers shared similar stories. At their lowest point God had used me to intercept and rescue them when no one else was awake. The very thing I had been praying for God to remove was the thing He would use to do an amazing work. When God doesn't work as we think He should, it does not mean He isn't working. It may just be that He has something far better in mind.

God *is* at work, even in the most unlikely places. Sometimes we may write off certain places or people or situations, thinking that God could never work there. But we would be so wrong!

---

20. That's what we used "back in the day."

GOD AT WORK IN A . . . PRISON?

Some members of our family have been on death row. Let's rephrase that. I (Tom) have visited one of the most infamous maximum security prisons in America. It was with my dad, and it was because of the study *Experiencing God*.

Louisiana State Penitentiary is "home" to about 5,200 men. Over 3,700 inmates are serving life sentences there for committing heinous crimes. The death penalty is legal in that state, so many are just waiting to be executed.

Let's back up a few years. The prison, more widely known as Angola Prison, was not a happy place. Brutality was the order of the day for many inmates. With an average sentence of eighty years, what did they have left to lose? Angola had the highest level of violence of any prison in America, but that was going to change.

When Burl Cain came on as the new warden, he was overwhelmed at the task before him. The first execution he oversaw brought home the sheer hopelessness of the place. He watched a man die in fear, without hope. Deeply shaken, Cain decided to offer the course *Experiencing God* to inmates. Taking the course was not mandatory, but God began to use the biblical truths in that study[21] to radically change lives. Before long, many of the men accepted Christ and found forgiveness for their sins. The corresponding change in their character was measurable: the violence level plummeted by

---

21. . . . which happen to be the same truths we are describing in this book.

73 percent! Other prison wardens began to ask Cain for his secret, and he told them.

Bible studies were offered in other prisons, with the same positive results. In fact, many of the initial converts from Angola requested a transfer to other highly violent institutions so they could be missionaries. They even started a seminary in Angola so inmates who sensed God's call into ministry (yes, you read that correctly) could receive theological training and become pastors within the prison walls. We met with numerous men on Death Row, and they radiated a joy that can only be explained by God's presence.[22]

Stories continue to flow from Angola, telling of radical life transformations as these men, most of whom society has forgotten, encounter God. God can work anywhere He wants, doing mighty things that can only be credited to Him. And that's exactly what He did at Angola. All it took was one humble warden who recognized that truth and acted on it.

God is always at work around you.

The question is, "Are you watching for Him?" You often only see what you're really looking for. This truth is so important for you to grasp in order to take the steps that are to follow. If you can't recognize God at work, then you will never be able to move forward in your relationship with Him.

---

22. You have not experienced the song "Amazing Grace" until you have heard a forgiven murderer sing, "Amazing grace, how sweet the sound, that saved a wretch like *me*!" at the top of his lungs!

WALKING WITH GOD

1. Where have you seen God at work around you lately? Have your eyes been open, or have you missed Him?

2. How can you actively be watching to see where God is at work? What are some habits you can develop that will help you be watchful?

3. What are some distractions in your life that hinder you from seeing God at work? What can you do about them?

4. Consider a time when you have thought, surely God is not at work there! What does the Bible say about when, where, and how God works? Are there any limits for Him?

2

GOD
PURSUES
A LOVE
RELATIONSHIP
WITH YOU

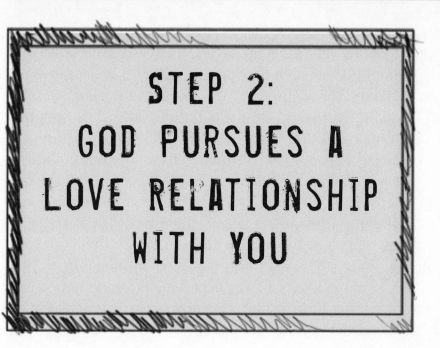

STEP 2:
GOD PURSUES A
LOVE RELATIONSHIP
WITH YOU

"Yes, I have loved you with an everlasting love; therefore with lovingkindness I have drawn you."
—*JEREMIAH 31:3 NKJV*

THAT CRAZY LITTLE THING CALLED LOVE

True love . . .

Can you think of any other two words that conjure up such irrepressible emotion?[23] A nineteenth-century writer, William Thackeray, rightly declared, "Love makes fools of us all,." One small drop of love can morph a grubby bachelor into a sensitive, cake-baking, flower-buying Romeo.

---

23. And no, "Dallas Cowboys" doesn't count.

Daniel has been an avid Buffalo Sabres fan since before he was able to wipe the saliva off his chin with a Buffalo Sabres spirit rag. He doesn't just cheer for the Buffalo Sabres. He lives the Buffalo Sabres. He watches every one of their games while eating popcorn out of a Buffalo Sabres bowl, drinking from a Buffalo Sabres mug, wearing a Buffalo Sabres jersey, and yelling out his favorite Buffalo Sabres cheers. He's traveled to seven different cities just to watch them play. Heck, he even eats buffalo-style wings. The fact that they've got about the same chance of winning a championship as the Amazon jungle has of experiencing a snow storm doesn't discourage him. He cheers with a fanatic fervor that borders on mental instability.

"WUV. TRUE WUV!"

In the 1987 movie *The Princess Bride*, a farmhand named Westley falls in love with the young woman of the house, Buttercup. Realizing he has nothing to offer her but hard work, he leaves to seek his fortune with the intention of returning to marry her.

His ship is attacked by the Dread Pirate Roberts. Roberts normally kills all the captives but is intrigued by the young man's quest and spares his life on account of "true love."

Thinking him to be dead, Buttercup agrees to marry the evil Prince Humperdinck. Throughout the movie Westley overcomes each and every challenge (a giant, a Spanish swordsman, an evil genius, a corrupt prince, various henchmen, and Rodents of Unusual Size in the fire swamp) that stand between him and his true love in order to win the hand of Buttercup in marriage. After all, love will make you do crazy things!

The great philosopher Plato knew well the power of love, which is what led to perhaps the most acute metaphysical thought of his career: Love is "madness." Love affects us all. Now before you check the front cover of this book and make sure you didn't pick up your mom's cheesy Harlequin romance novel by mistake, let us explain the reason for this "love talk." Here it is: Without a proper understanding of what true love actually is, you will be unable to fully appreciate this next step:

Truth #2: God pursues a continuing love relationship with you that is real and personal.

This truth comes in two essential parts: love and relationship. Both make (or at least should make) a world of difference in the way we live. God does not just call us into a relationship; He calls us into a *love* relationship. Likewise, God does not just love us from afar; He shares that love through relationship. Do you see how the two work together?

However there's a fatal problem. Our understanding and model of love has become Hollywood-ized and watered down to a point where we no longer appreciate what God is offering us when He gives us His love.

So let's try to clarify. . . .

THE TRUTH ABOUT LOVE

There are only two kinds of love in this world.[24] The first is the love God created from the beginning of time. Then there's the fake love that Satan offers by corrupting what God created. First, let's have a quick look at this fake love. It's easy to spot because you see it around you every day. Just flip on the TV, go to the theater, browse the grocery store tabloids, or stop by a junior high school dance!

Here are some tried-and-true truths of TV love:

TV Love

 Love is something you "make."[25] You don't actually need to love someone to make love with them. In fact, you don't even have to be friends with your "love partner" as long as you're having fun. Oh, and don't fret about potential emotional or physical consequences—James Bond has survived fifty years of movies without any, right?

 Love is temporary. You love someone for a while. But when you get sick of each other or they turn out to be different than you expected (*gasp!*), you break up (best done by Facebook or text message). If you can fall in love, then of course you can fall out of love too. You should move on faster than you can say Kardashian.

---

24. And we don't just mean "guy love" and "gift love," regardless of how different they may seem!
25. Yes . . . we're talking about the *s-word*.

Love is just a word. When you say, "I love you," you mean it—of course, you also really love fuzzy slippers, your iPhone, the beach on a hot day, and extra bacon on your Big Mac.

 Love is for sharing. It's crazy to think that someone with so much love should be with only one person at a time! Go ahead and have a couple boyfriends or girlfriends simultaneously—as long as they don't find out about each other (Team Edward or Team Jacob). Spread the joy! Loyalty is for gangs and sports teams.

TRUE LOVE IS NOT THE SAME AS:

Lust
Sex
Like
Affection
Fondness
Friendship
Desire
Adoration
Worship
Care for
Respect
Admiration
Having feelings for

THE GREATEST HOCKEY PLAYER WHO NEVER LIVED!

In 2010 the trading card company Panini America released a new featured card for the player Taro Tsujimoto.

There's just one catch: Tsujimoto never existed!

As the 1974 NHL draft dragged on, one general manager grew restless. With the 183rd pick he announced his team's selection of Tsujimoto, a can't-miss prospect for the Tokyo Katanas. He then watched as the other scouts franticly searched for information on the fictional team and fictional player.

Even more crazy? Tons of people are buying it! Tsujimoto's card regularly sells for as much as fifty dollars a card! Not a bad profit for something that's not even real!

Counterfeit Love

The only problem with TV love is that it's *fake*. Have you ever traveled abroad or walked the streets of a big city like New York? It's amazing the kind of shopping deals you can find. The shady looking character in the dark alley is selling Oakley sunglasses or a Louis Vuitton purse for just five dollars!

Spoiler alert: They probably aren't real.

Knockoffs are cheap and easy to find if you know where to look. They may grab your attention and satisfy for a moment, but in the end they're still phony and almost worthless. They don't last. And you miss out on the real thing. That's Satan's gimmick.

"The Devil . . . was a murderer from the beginning and has not stood in the truth, because there is no truth in him. When he tells a lie, he speaks from his own nature, because he is a liar and the father of liars" (John 8:44).

From the beginning of time, Satan has counterfeited all the good things God created. Because of who he is, everything he touches becomes corrupt. Sometimes his substitutes for the genuine article turn out to be not only bogus but addictive and destructive. His enticing offers have great face appeal—get high, escape your problems, become more popular, achieve higher grades, pay less money, pay nothing at all, grab some thrills, grab bigger thrills, achieve wealth, fame, and power—but his promises are meant to be broken. That's what he does. And he keeps his customers coming back for more, because they are never satisfied.

UNDERSTANDING THE REAL THING

It's been said that when a bank is training new employees to recognize a counterfeit dollar they don't actually show them any forged bills. Instead they give them a real dollar bill. They let them feel it. Examine it. Smell it. The bankers become so familiar with the real thing that when they come across a counterfeit bill they immediately discern that it's a worthless replica.

> Love is patient,
> love is kind.
> Love does not envy,
> is not boastful,
> is not conceited,
> does not act improperly,
> is not selfish,
> is not provoked,
> and does not keep a record of wrongs.
> Love finds no joy in unrighteousness
> but rejoices in the truth.
> It bears all things,
> believes all things,
> hopes all things,
> endures all things.
> Love never ends.
> —1 Corinthians 13:4-8

The best way to recognize false love is to know what true love is. When you experience God's satisfying love, Satan's hollow promises lose their appeal.

When God says He loves us deeply, He means it. Not only that, but He proves it. The reason we even think about Him in the first place is because from the time we were born God has been demonstrating His love. Romans 5:8 says, "But God proves His own love for us in that while we were still sinners, Christ died for us!" There has never been a time in our lives when we were completely alone. God has always been with us—every moment of every day. He has been at work to help us understand His deep love for us personally.

EXTRAORDINARY LOVE

Are you familiar with the biblical story of Moses?[26] The moment Moses was born, his life was in danger. Pharaoh had ordered that all male babies born to the Israelites be put to death out of fear that his slaves were growing too strong and would attempt to overthrow their owners. But God had a plan in mind to use Moses some eighty years later.

Moses' mother made a covered basket from reeds and sent her newborn floating down the Nile River—in God's hands. Ironically, Pharaoh's own daughter found the basket, adopted the baby, and Moses grew up eating at the table with the very people who ordered his death.

Over the course of his life, Moses knew what it was like to be pampered, and he also found out what it feels like to be an outcast, hiding out for his life from the law. During this time, he had several momentous encounters with God. We'll let you read about them for yourself, but probably the best known is the burning bush. It's a fascinating account of Moses encountering God in a bush

---

26. His story is found in the book of Exodus.

that was on fire but was not being consumed by the flames.[27]

Ultimately, Moses became the leader of his nation and no one was more surprised by that than he was. He was a highly unlikely candidate for the job. He battled anxiety, he was a lousy speaker, he lacked courage, he had a quick temper, and he lacked self control. But God chose him to decimate the mighty Egyptian army. The mere mention of Moses' name would bring fear into the hearts of the people inhabiting the Promised Land.

God was there when Moses was born, when he was adopted, when he went into exile, when he led the slaves out of Egypt, and God was there when Moses' life came to an end at 120 years old (Deuteronomy 34:4–7).

It is no different for you. God was there at your birth. He watched as you learned to walk. He heard your first words. Saw the first picture you colored. Smiled when you finally learned to ride a bike. Just like He saw Moses at his best and his worst, the same God has seen your disappointments, your victories, and He knows your hopes and dreams.

The bottom line is this: He wants you to know and experience His amazing love.

---

27. Funny story: The original *Experiencing God* book cover has an artist's portrayal of Moses during this encounter: long beard, staff, and robe. When a dear old lady met Henry for the first time, she exclaimed, "Wow, you look *nothing* like the cover of your book!"

STAIRS OF DOOM

 My family and I (Tom) had enjoyed our few days in the beautiful city of Salzburg.[28] I had gone upstairs in our bed-and-breakfast to retrieve one last suitcase when I heard a bloodcurdling scream come from the stairwell. I instantly recognized it—it was my one-year-old son, Conor.

As I ran toward the bedroom door, my oldest son Matt came in holding his baby brother in his arms. Blood was streaming down Conor's face. He had fallen down the stairs and gashed his forehead on a large ceramic pot. We wiped away the blood and found a huge slash from his forehead through his eyebrow.

I quickly carried him down the stairs to the receptionist. Not knowing any German, I simply pointed to the still-bleeding wound. I had absolutely no idea where to go or who to call. She pointed out the front door—there was a medical clinic just across the street! The nurse there didn't speak English, but she saw (and heard) us coming and motioned that we were going to be next in line regardless of who was waiting ahead of us.

Moments later, the examining doctor took one look at Conor and gestured that his clinic was not equipped to handle such a deep cut. We were instructed to go to the hospital immediately. I had no idea how to even find a hospital.

There I was in a foreign country with my son

---

28. Yes, Salzburg of *Sound of Music* fame!

depending on me, and I had absolutely no clue how to even ask for directions! But I knew how to pray.

After an ambulance ride and numerous forms to fill out (in German) we discovered that there just happened to be a renowned plastic surgeon in residence. Conor has a hairline scar that's barely visible today. Believe me, few situations feel as helpless as when you're a dad in a strange country holding a bleeding, howling baby. But God was watching over us, and He walked with us through the whole ordeal. How grateful I am to know that God loves us through every trial we face.

GOD'S LOVE IS IN A LEAGUE OF ITS OWN

Fortunately, God's love isn't like TV love or any other counterfeit form of love. It's pure and true and never-ending. This is what God—the Creator of love and the Creator of you—tells us about His love. Accept no substitutes.

God means what He says. So when God says "I love you," He means it. He told His people *"I have loved you with an everlasting love; therefore with lovingkindness I have drawn you"* (JEREMIAH 31:3 NKJV). God's love is the genuine article, and He always has our best interests in mind. When we let God in, His love will fill that empty spot in our life perfectly, so that we feel complete just as God created us to be. Let's be real here. Perhaps you have sought this love somewhere else.[29]

---

29. This can often take the form of sex or pornography for guys, who mistake pleasure for love. Girls often seek love by giving themselves fully to a guy in hopes that he will give her love and self-worth in return, even if the guy is actually a total jerk.

② *God's love is permanent.* It's loyal, focused, and determined. When we disappoint God, He loves us. When we sin, He loves us still and offers forgiveness. When we deliberately reject Him, He still loves us and keeps graciously drawing us back to Himself. Aren't you glad that God is more patient with us than we often are with each other?

There's no place you can go and nothing you can do that is outside of God's love for you. King David said, "God will never break his promise to me. God's promise is complete and unchanging; he will always help me and give me what I hope for" (2 Samuel 23:5 CEV). God's

A LOVE STORY: FEATURING A PIG AND A FROG

In the 2011 movie *The Muppets*, Kermit the Frog comes to the realization that the love of one important person is better than all other cheap imitations. For him, this takes the form of the "beautiful" Miss Piggy. In a touching scene, he says, "Maybe you don't need the whole world to love you. Maybe you just need one person." As Christians, we get our self-worth from God's love alone. There are all sorts of counterfeit loves out there that you will be tempted to put your hope in, but none of them compare to the love of God. That alone is unique.

love is not a gold star that can be awarded or taken away. It's there for good.

 God's love is all-powerful. No force is greater than the Father's love, no person stronger, no situation too tough that God's love will not prevail on our behalf. "No, in all these things we are more than victorious through Him who loved us. For I am persuaded that not even death or life, angels or rulers, things present or things to come, hostile powers, height or depth, or any other created thing will have the power to separate us from the love of God that is in Christ Jesus our Lord!" (Romans 8:37–39).

Isn't it amazing how Jesus describes His protection of us? "No one will snatch them out of My hand. My Father, who has given them to Me, is greater than all. No one is able to snatch them out of the Father's hand. The Father and I are one" (John 10:28–30). When you understand that God wants to have a love relationship with you, understand also what kind of love He is talking about.

ONE MINUTE TO LIVE

Chris had been planning the day for quite some time. He never thought he would actually go through with it—but today was the day. He was tired of his life. Tired of fighting addictions. Tired of feeling not good enough. Tired of feeling defective. It had been this way ever since his dad had left.

He had held the pistol in his hand before and remembered just how heavy it felt. He knew it was loaded; it was always loaded. The steel felt cold. A quick thought about what his mother would do when she found him flashed through his mind, but disappeared with the sound of the hammer locking into place. As he raised the gun toward his head, he was stopped by the sound of someone knocking at the front door.

He laid the gun down on the bed, closed the bedroom door, and went downstairs to open the door. It was his youth pastor. "Hey Chris, I was in the area, and I just felt like stopping by. What's going on with you today?" One minute later and Chris would have been dead.

Today, we are pleased to say, Chris is happily married with two beautiful daughters and serves in the United States military defending his country. God sent his pastor to stop him from making a terrible mistake. Chris needed to know that God still loved him, and that knowledge was enough for him to put the gun down. When you know that your heavenly Father loves you, it can mean the difference between life and death.

SO HOW DO I KNOW GOD LOVES ME?

First, take your Bible out and flip over to Luke, chapter 23, and read through it. Take your time; don't rush through. Or put in Mel Gibson's movie *The Passion of the Christ*. As you read or watch the suffering Christ endured, just tell yourself that He was doing it all for you.

Christ had done nothing wrong. He lived a perfect life completely pleasing to God. But God "laid on him the sins of us all" (Isaiah 53:6 NLT). He was paying the penalty for you. He willingly laid down His life as a sacrifice so that if you trust Him and repent of your sins, you would find forgiveness and you could have eternal life from that moment on.

We have heard many people say, "I just don't feel like God loves me." It is a dangerous thing to go through life based on your emotions. God's love for us is not based on our feelings; it is established on truth. We're so glad the promises of God in the Bible don't fluctuate from day to day based on how we feel. The Bible says, *"For God so loved the world . . ."* (JOHN 3:16 KJV), and that does not change. Ever.

BUT WAIT, THERE'S MORE!

Before Jesus was crucified, He explained to His disciples what was going to happen after the cross. He made an extremely important promise to them:

"Nevertheless, I am telling you the truth. It is for your benefit that I go away, because if I don't go away the Counselor will not come to you. If I go, I will send Him to you." (JOHN 16:7)

"But the Counselor, the Holy Spirit—the Father will send Him in My name—will teach you all things and remind you of everything I have told you." (JOHN 14:26)

That promise is for you as well. Jesus prayed this for you: "I pray not only for these, but also for those who believe in Me through their message. . . . May they be made completely one, so the world may know You have sent Me and have loved them as You have loved Me" (John 17:20, 23). God will never leave you on your own. He promises that His Spirit will be with you all the time to protect you, guide you, teach you, strengthen you, and remind you of His constant love for you. This is His "deposit," guaranteeing that you belong to Him and that one day He will return.

God has made you lots of other promises too.

 He promises to provide protection for those who call upon Him in time of need. [Psalm 91]

 He promises direction for when we need it. [Proverbs 16:9, Psalm 31:3]

 He promises blessings when we follow His commands. [Proverbs 10:6, 28:20]

 He promises comfort in times of sorrow and grief. [Psalm 23:4, 94:19]

The Old Testament tells about a seasoned war veteran named Joshua. He was an army general who had been with Moses. After Moses died, it was Joshua's turn to lead the Israelites through exceedingly difficult times, and God did amazing things through Joshua just as He did through Moses. Joshua had a trust in God that never wavered. Before he died, this faithful servant delivered a powerful speech to his countrymen. Here is one of the things he told them: "I am now going the way of all the earth, and you know with all your heart and all your soul that none of the good promises the Lord your God made to you has failed. Everything was fulfilled for you; not one promise has failed" (Joshua 23:14).

After reminding the people of God's faithfulness to them, Joshua challenged them about how they would respond: He said, *"Choose for yourselves today the one you will worship. . . . As for me and my family, we will worship Yahweh"* (Joshua 24:15).

We'd like to close this chapter with the same reminder and the same challenge.

If you are already a believer in Jesus as your Lord and Savior, you are on an exciting journey. God has promised to show you the pathway through life. You know He loves you deeply, because He gave His life for you. It's your decision how you will respond to God's love.

WALKING WITH GOD

1. List five ways God has showed you He loves you.

2. Remember Chris, the guy we told you about who almost committed suicide? Do you know of a time when God intervened in your life to save you from doing something stupid that could have had disasterous consequences?

3. The Bible says the way we treat others reflects our love for God. Think about the way you behave toward your family members, your friends, your classmates, teachers, and so on. What does that say about your view of what love really is?

4. Jesus said, "I assure you: Whatever you did for one of the least of these brothers of Mine, you did for Me" (Matthew 25:40). What is one specific action you could take today to care for someone in need?

5. Have you bought into the lie of TV love? What things in your life need to change if you desire to exchange that love for real love?

3

GOD INVITES YOU TO BECOME INVOLVED WITH HIM IN HIS WORK

STEP 3: GOD INVITES YOU TO BECOME INVOLVED WITH HIM IN HIS WORK

"'Follow Me,' He told them, 'and I will make you fish for people!' Immediately they left their nets and followed Him."—MATTHEW 4:19–20

THE MAKING OF A ROCK STAR

Mike's friend Brad had always dreamed of becoming a rock star. He played trumpet in his high school band, but his real passion was only unleashed when making sweet noise through his trusty ol' Fender. He patiently bided his time, waiting for the stars to align to fulfill his destiny. When that moment finally arrived, it came from the most unlikely of places. . . .

His sister's best friend had gotten front row tickets to a Relient K concert and wanted to take her dad and her best friend (Brad's sister). In a strange twist of fate (or perhaps musical preference), the girl's dad encouraged her to give the ticket to someone else who might like to go, someone with a car. Brad had a car.

Call it luck, serendipity, begging, whatever; she asked Brad to go to the concert. He excitedly donned his faded blue jeans and tight gray shirt (because nothing says "rock 'n' roll" like some good sweat stains) and headed to the concert.

They made their way to the very front row. The lights went down and Relient K finally burst onstage. The place was electric! Lights, guitars, drums, fans, body odor—it was everything a music fan could hope for. Or was it?

The lead singer addressed the crowd and called upon a fan to come onstage and play guitar with them for one song. There was only one person in the audience who was right for the job. Without waiting for an invitation, Brad began making his way backstage. About halfway there, he locked eyes with the lead singer. The look said, "I know it's me. You know it's me. Let us fulfill our destinies together." He ducked under the barrier, greeted the security guy with a nod, and strapped on the provided guitar. Then they called him on stage.

There he was. Once a spectator—now a spectacle. The concert was in his hometown, so Brad could look out in the crowd and see familiar faces, knowing their relationship could never be the same after his catapult to stardom. They started the song and he waited for his part.

When it came time for him to join in, he fell to one knee under the weight of the rock 'n' roll screaming out of his guitar. When the song ended, the crowd flew into a frenzy. Brad lifted his arms to show his appreciation.

The stains under his arms proved what he already knew: he rocked. Hard. He exited stage left by giving a ninja-style high kick from the top of the stage to the floor. He nearly twisted an ankle, but in that moment he was invincible. He made his way back to the front row, returning as one who had successfully navigated a rite of passage into manhood. He was a rock star, and he was never even supposed to be there.

THE MASTER PIANIST

Legend tells of a mother whose young boy grudgingly took piano lessons. However, he continually refused to practice.

To inspire him, she decided to take him to a concert performance by the great classical musician Ignace Jan Paderewski.

Waiting for the concert to begin, the mother turned to chat with friends. When the lights dimmed she realized in horror that her boy had wandered off.

Just then the curtains parted. Sitting at the piano onstage was her son. He began plucking out the tune of "*Twinkle, Twinkle Little Star.*" The crowd was silent as Paderewski slowly approached the boy. He leaned over the boy and whispered, "Good job. Just keep playing."

Then reached his arms around and began playing a complex counter-melody. His hands danced up and down the keys as the little guy steadily plucked out the tune.

By the time the last note was played, the duo received a fervent standing ovation.

INVITED

That was an unforgettable moment for Brad, and Mike was genuinely happy for his buddy (which is not to say he wasn't as green as the Grinch with envy). The band certainly didn't need Brad in order to play their show, but they invited him to join in; it was their gift to him.

Have you ever wondered why God would need our help to touch the world? After all, He's God, and we're mere mortals. People ask that question all the time. The short answer is that He doesn't need us by any means. But He invites us so we can have a small part in the experience along with Him. Brad could not even find the words to describe how much he enjoyed playing in that concert. Likewise, just seeing God at work is a really big deal, but actually being a part of His activity is that much better.

The difference between being a spectator and being a participant is huge. God knows this. That's why we have the next truth:

Truth #3:

God invites you to become involved with Him in His work.

DWIGHT LYMAN MOODY

You may have heard of D. L. Moody, one of the greatest evangelists of all time. What you may not know is his humble beginnings. Moody's father died when he was just four years old. His family had no money, and when his father died, the creditors took everything (even the firewood!). He and his seven siblings would carry their shoes to church to keep them from getting worn out. His total education was no more than five years of primary school, his writing was barely legible, and his use of grammar was atrocious.

But then Jesus saved him, and any man's life in the hands of God is a powerful tool. Later in his life, a critic told Moody that he should not speak publicly, since he made so many mistakes in grammar. Moody replied, "I know I make mistakes, and I lack many things, but I am doing the best I can with what I've got. Look here, friend, you've got grammar enough. What are you doing with it for Jesus?" Moody knew that it was not about your abilities but your obedience to God that made all the difference. And what a difference he made! Few preachers in this world have had a greater impact than D. L. Moody.

Taken from James S. Bell Jr., *The D. L. Moody Collection.*

How can we grasp the weight of that truth? God's magnum opus stretches across the entire globe. It involves millions of people and billions of tiny threads— all coming together to form one grand masterpiece. And He wants to include you.

Henry Blackaby (by now you must know that's Tom's dad and Mike/Dan's grandpa) is a man of few words (except when he is preaching, that is). He's a soft-spoken, humble, ordinary man. Yet, he has prayed with presidents in the Oval Office and counseled world leaders in other countries. As we said earlier, Henry has also been in maximum security prisons and prayed with condemned convicts.

When he shares those stories with us, his face lights up, and you can hear the wonder in his voice. He tells about an elderly inmate on death row who closed his eyes and sang "Amazing Grace" in perfect pitch as a way to express the joy in his heart because of Jesus. Or another prisoner who weaves simple cross necklaces as a testimony about the love of Christ. Henry has several paintings and other pieces of art created by all sorts of people from all over the world. It's their way of trying to express what God has done in their lives. But as we said, words are inadequate to describe what it's like to walk closely with God and to be part of His life-changing work.

Throughout history God has invited men and women to be part of carrying out His divine plans. Moses, Gideon, Joshua, Abraham, Samuel, David, Hannah, Ruth, Rebekah, Mary (actually more than one Mary), Martha, and the list goes on . . . (insert your name here).

CALLED TO SOMETHING SCARY

We are all a little scared that God will ask us to do something we feel inadequate to do. Carrie (Mike and Dan's younger sister) was so afraid to be called on in her college classes that she developed an impressive array of diversions just in case. She always sat directly behind the biggest football player. She pretended to be looking up textbook references to avoid eye contact with the professor. She dropped pens and lip balms with regularity so she could bend down out of sight. She would fake a nasty cough that relayed "sore throat, no voice." Finally her professor told her, "Carrie, you're a bright girl, and you know the material. I'm on to all your tricks, and I will call on you, so be ready."

What if God asks us to join Him in something we don't like to do? What if we're caught unprepared? What if He asks us to do something we can't do?

Want the truth?

He will do that. Look in the Bible; it's God's M.O.

Moses was the poster boy for being-called-on-by-God-but-feeling-inadequate. He was a fugitive because in a fit of temper he had murdered an Egyptian. That led to him hiding out for forty years in the backside of the desert shepherding "flocks," which is a pretty word for nasty goats. Then one day God spoke to him and sent him, of all places, back to Egypt. And he wasn't just sent home; he was sent home to undertake a terrifying, unthinkable mission. God told Moses to demand that the most powerful man in the world (the Pharaoh) set his entire labor force free to go worship an unknown God in the desert. Can you imagine what went on in Moses' head? Not in a million years would Moses have manufactured that idea on his own. But that's what was on God's heart.

That's what God does. He finds us even as we're trying to make ourselves invisible and gives us an assignment that's beyond the scope of our imagination.

NO ARMS, NO LEGS, NO WORRIES

Nick Vujicic felt God's call to be an evangelist. The only problem was he suffered from tetra-amelia syndrome: he was born with no arms or legs. How could he be a public speaker? Surely God had asked the wrong man.

To date he has shared the gospel with more than three million people in twenty-four different countries.

What's God calling you to do? Take it from Nick: God is much bigger than anything that you think is holding you back.

GOD'S AGENDA

All through the grand narrative of Scripture, we see God repeatedly inviting men and women to leave what they were doing and join Him in His plans.

Without exception, His agenda is broader than our own. Our ideas may be less terrifying or even more fun, but God's ways are higher than our ways, and His thoughts are higher than our thoughts (Isaiah 55:9).

He can accomplish more than we could ever even think to ask (Ephesians 3:20). So, which is wiser: to come up with a master plan and ask God to bless it, or to ask Him for His agenda and follow that instead?

It's so straightforward. Yet, we get it backward all the time. Even Christian leaders do. They come up with a grand idea and then mobilize their followers to go for it, with the hope that God has their back. That's totally unbiblical. In fact, the Bible has a great word for choosing our own plans over God's—*stupidity*. (Well, the word in Proverbs is *folly*, but that's what it means.)

In the Scriptures it's always God bringing people into His plan for His purposes.

As you start to recognize that God is constantly at work around you, and as you come to know Him in an intimate love relationship, you will grow increasingly sensitive to what is on His heart and where He wants to take you. It may be nothing like what you would have planned for yourself—and that's good news. Being used by God to accomplish His will is unlike anything else you will ever do.

AN EARLY WAKE-UP CALL

Rhonda had been attending Mike and Dan's church for several weeks. She was curious about God but didn't know if she was ready to give her life to Him. One night, Heather, a woman in the church, called and invited her to a Sunday afternoon small group she was hosting. It was designed for people like Rhonda who wanted to know more about the Bible. But Rhonda was going to be busy that day, since she was heading out of town for work all week. She graciously declined.

The next morning Heather woke up at 4:45 a.m. She was wide awake and felt compelled to pray for Rhonda immediately. So, getting out of bed, she dropped to her knees and prayed.

As she prayed, the Lord directed her to call Rhonda. It was 4:55 a.m.—and she barely knew this woman. The idea seemed ridiculous, but Heather looked up Rhonda's number and keyed it into her phone. She let it ring three times before she hastily hung up. "There," she thought, "at least I tried!" But she sensed an urgency that prompted her to call again. This time—Rhonda answered.

Heather quickly explained that she didn't normally call anyone at that hour but told her what had happened. There was a pause and then Rhonda said, "Okaaay." Then Heather told her that God loved her and asked Rhonda if she could pray for her over the phone and ask the Lord to watch over her as she traveled that day. Rhonda agreed, and then they each said goodbye.

Heather felt like an idiot. It was so not her usual style, and she felt completely awkward! But the next Sunday, out of the blue, Rhonda showed up ten minutes before the Bible study at Heather's house. Heather immediately started in on an apology, but Rhonda replied, "No, that's why I came. I needed to tell you something. Right before you called, I was in the shower, and I prayed for the first time in my life. I said, 'God, if You're there, forgive my sins.' The reason I didn't say much on the phone was because I was in shock. God prompted you to call me at the very time I needed His assurance. And that's why I'm here now." Rhonda was later baptized on Easter Sunday.

GOD AT WORK

God had already been at work in Rhonda's life, and He wanted Heather to be a part of it. It was God's way of pointing to her from onstage and saying, "Okay, Heather, you're up!" Although she didn't know all the details, and it seemed strange at the time, Heather was obedient. As a result, both Heather and Rhonda got to experience God that early morning.

So what might God do in and through your life? The famous evangelist D.L. Moody was once challenged by something his friend Henry Varley said: "The world has yet to see what God can do with a man fully consecrated to him." Those words struck Moody to the heart, and he made a commitment: "By God's help, I aim to be that man."

It is estimated that one million souls were saved as a direct result of his ministry. What could God do in and through your life, if you would decide right now to join Him where He is working?

You see, recognizing where God is at work is only part of the story; joining Him is the other part.

BE ON WATCH

How do you know when God is at work and wanting you to join Him? One important thing to do is to watch. What you do after you pray is vitally important. When you say, "God, reveal to me where You are at work so I can join You," you have to watch for an answer. If you're not looking for it, you could miss God's answer to your prayer.

In Luke, chapter 19, you'll find the account of a man named Zacchaeus. He was detested because of his job as

a tax collector. Zacchaeus was not very tall, so when he heard that Jesus was passing through town, he was so determined to see Him that he climbed a sycamore tree to see over the mob.[30]

Jesus was surrounded by crowds on all sides, but He spotted Zacchaeus and called out to him: "Zacchaeus, hurry and come down because today I must stay at your house" (Luke 19:5). Why did Jesus say He must do that? Because He knew that the Father was at work in Zacchaeus's life.

We know that Jesus spent much time in prayer (Mark 1:35). If you want to know what God is doing right where you are, seek Him in prayer and then watch for the opportunity to join Him. Often these opportunities come in ways you would least expect.

---

30. We had the opportunity to visit Israel and see the actual tree (at least that's what the tour guide wanted us to think!) that he climbed. But be warned: if you ever get this opportunity, you'll be tempted to climb the tree yourself—just to get away from the people trying to sell you cheap postcards!

A WORD FROM GOD

As a young man Augustine reveled in all sorts of sexual and reckless sin. He was familiar with the Bible but viewed it as simply an ancient book of teachings.

Until one day, in his mid-thirties, he heard a child singing a simple song with the lyrics, "Pick it up and read it. Pick it up and read it." He had never heard that song before.

He went straight home and grabbed his Bible. He opened it up and read the first passage he saw.

Let us walk with decency, as in the daylight: not in carousing and drunkenness; not in sexual impurity and promiscuity; not in quarreling and jealousy. But put on the Lord Jesus Christ, and make no plans to satisfy the fleshly desires.—ROMANS 13:13–14

Augustine gave his life to Christ and is widely considered to be one of the most important thinkers in Church history.

Taken from Sherwood E. Writ, *The Confessions of Augustine in Modern English*.

A WEDDING TO REMEMBER

I (Mike) will never forget the first wedding I officiated as a pastor. In fact, it was a special wedding that everyone who attended is not likely to forget. Here's what happened.

On a Sunday morning, a single mother in our church introduced me to her daughter Stacy and Stacy's boyfriend John. They were nice kids, and we hit it off right away. I invited them to check out the Bible study I was teaching. I also told them about the Thursday night coffeehouse our young-adult group hosted in a café down the street from our church. They began to periodically attend both, and I developed a relationship with them.

Before long, the three of them needed help moving, and I agreed to help them. Several other guys from our church pitched in too. It became obvious that John and Stacy were living together. They shared one bedroom, and Stacy's mom had the other. This made me pretty uncomfortable, but what was I to do? I'm notoriously nonconfrontational, so the thought of bringing up their situation terrified me. But I also had a strong sense that God was at work in the life of this young couple. So I prayed. I basically said, "God, if this is a conversation you want me to have, please provide the opportunity to have it." I didn't need to wait long.

The next day, I got a call at almost midnight from this couple. Their car had broken down an hour outside of town, and they were stranded. I jumped in my car and headed down the highway to pick them up. I was now looking at spending an hour with this couple in my car with their undivided attention. I had my answer.

As we drove back, I said, "Guys, I know you want God to bless your relationship. The thing is, He is not going to bless your relationship unless you first honor Him with it. To do that, you've got a couple options. You can either 1) have one of you move out, or 2) get married."

A brief, uncomfortable silence followed, but then Stacy broke the tension. "We've planned on getting married for a while now, and even had a date set, but we can't afford it, so we've been putting it off. Are you qualified to marry us?"

I was taken aback. I myself was not married and had never conducted a wedding before. The story had taken an unexpected turn. I answered, "Um, yeah, I think I am. Let me look into it."

After dropping them off, I prayed, "God, what is Your plan in all of this?"

Then it hit me. *Marry them at the coffeehouse on a Thursday night.*

These evenings, called "Café on Main," are pretty informal; people come to enjoy a cup of coffee, a band plays Christian music, and I usually share a message. It's the most eclectic group of people I've ever had the privilege to be a part of, with every imaginable ethnicity, background, and personality coming each week. But have a wedding there? It was crazy, but I couldn't deny it was an idea from God. So I pitched the idea to the couple, and they loved it. Our group would put together the wedding; all they needed to pay for was the marriage license.

I divvied out assignments to various people in our group, and in two weeks we planned a full-blown wedding at our café![31] And what a wedding it was! They didn't have many friends or family to attend, but the room was filled

---

31. Thus showing every Bridezilla that yes, you can indeed plan a wedding for cheap without thirty-four stressful months of preparation!

to capacity with the regular café crowd whom they had come to know in the preceding weeks (several who came had no idea we were even doing a wedding that evening).

We were able to fly the groom's mom in from Oregon. Someone in the church made the cake; someone else provided flowers. A lady loaned us her chocolate fountain. Others decorated the tables and brought food. We set up a beautiful archway, our band provided the music, a friend filmed the whole thing, and someone did a wedding photo shoot. We had a guest book, gifts, and party favors. The bride was beaming (actually, so was the groom). I can honestly say it was one of the best weddings I have been to.[32]

Not too long after that, the happy couple moved to Portland, Oregon, to be near his family. I later got an e-mail from them with a picture of the young adult Sunday school class they had become involved with in their new church. They were doing well and couldn't be happier. What did I learn from this experience? I learned that God is working in the hearts of people, and if we have our spiritual eyes open, we can be involved in some pretty amazing ways.

I wasn't looking for that opportunity. In fact, I wanted to avoid it altogether. But God was at work in Stacy and John's life. He brought us together, and as I was sensitive to seek the heart of God, it became very obvious to me what I was to do. Each step I took revealed more of God's plan, and now I can look back with fond memories of how God used me to draw a spiritually drifting couple back into His arms. It was better than anything I could have come up with. But then again, God's plans usually are.

---

32. And I'll just be honest: I don't normally enjoy weddings.

WILL YOU JOIN HIM?

God is working, and He wants you to join Him. So what might God be calling you to do? Have you spent time in prayer seeking His will in this way? Have you had your spiritual eyes open to see the answers to your prayers? Don't just pray; watch and pray (Mark 14:38). Don't miss out on any opportunity to join God at work.

An obedient Christian should never be bored. The problem is not that there is nothing to do; the problem is that many of us are too busy (or too lazy) or afraid to do it. Or in many cases people simply don't know how to get onto God's agenda.

The hope is that the deeper we get into this book, the more clearly you understand that God has much on His heart to accomplish all around you. He invites you to join Him, and when you do (take our word for it) boredom will not be a problem for you.

So are you ready to join God in what He is doing?

We will leave you with this scene from *The Chronicles of Narnia:*

> *"Please, Aslan! Am I not to know?"*
>
> *"To know what would have happened, child?"* said Aslan. *"No, nobody is ever told that."*
>
> *"Oh dear," said Lucy.*
>
> *"But anyone can find out what will happen,"* said Aslan. *"If you go back to the others now, and wake them up; and tell them you have seen me again; and that you must all get up at once and follow me—what will happen? There is only one way of finding out."*[33]

---

33. C. S. Lewis, *Prince Caspian* (New York: Macmillan Publishing Company, 1951), 137–38.

WALKING WITH GOD

1. Think of a time when you saw God at work. Did you join Him? What were the results?

2. What is it that normally keeps you from joining God at work? Is it that you don't notice where He is working? Is it because you're afraid it might take you out of your comfort zone?

3. What might you miss by not joining God at work?

4. Have you ever had God answer your prayer with a plan that greatly exceeded what you were expecting? Jot down what happened.

GOD SPEAKS BY THE HOLY SPIRIT

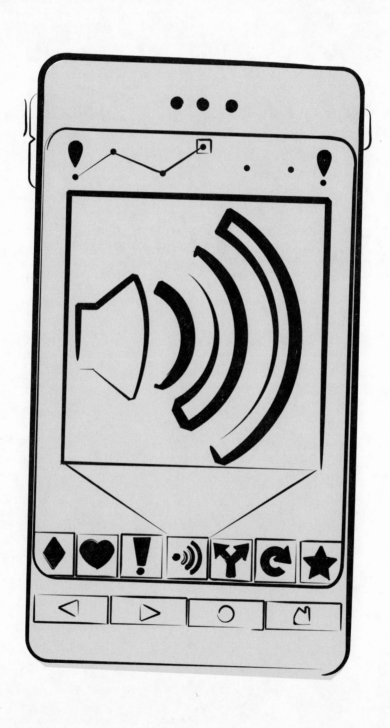

STEP 4: GOD SPEAKS BY THE HOLY SPIRIT

"And many nations will come and say, 'Come, let us go up to the mountain of the LORD, to the house of the God of Jacob. He will teach us about His ways so we may walk in His paths.'"—MICAH 4:2

RISE AND SHINE

I (Mike) am not a morning person. I do not enjoy rising before the sun to go for a jog, eat a healthy breakfast, or read the newspaper while the rest of the world sleeps. I prefer to hit the snooze button on my alarm as many times as I can . . . and then once more. My breakfast consists of the granola bar I grab on my way out the door. I get my exercise by running to my car, and I catch up on world events by tuning in to my car radio. Despite my unhealthy morning habits, however, I can always rely on my trusted alarm clock. Or so I thought. . . .

In 2008, I had the opportunity to speak in Singapore with my father. My dad is a world traveler with thousands of miles under his belt. Me? Not as much. I clearly remember the talk he gave me the night before we left for the airport. Like most international flights, they know you have plenty of time to sleep on the airplane (despite being sandwiched between two extremely large people, having no leg room, and being assaulted by the sound of four crying babies) so they always make the departure time as early as possible. On this particular flight, that time was 6:45 a.m. Since we lived forty-five minutes away from the airport and needed to clear long customs and security lines, our meeting time was 0400.

"Mike," he told me, "Make sure you are *in my driveway* at four o'clock in the morning. That doesn't mean 'leaving your apartment at four.' It means 'in my car pulling out of my driveway at four.'" I assured him that, as a twenty-three-year-old man, I was a responsible adult and refused his offer to give me a wake-up call.

I abruptly awoke the next morning to the annoying sound of my cell phone. As I scrambled to answer it, my eyes darted to my alarm clock. It read 4:05. My dad is going to eat me. After a rather short and somewhat direct conversation with my father, I proceeded to run around my room throwing anything I could find into a suitcase. I flew out the door and raced to my parent's house, screeching into their driveway, where my dad was waiting, car started and trunk open.

I jumped in the front seat. "Did you remember your passport?" he asked. Oh no. This was going to be a long morning—or a short life!

Truth #4:
God speaks by the Holy Spirit through the Bible, prayer, circumstances, and the church to reveal Himself, His purposes and His ways.

GOD SPEAKS

What does it take to get your attention? If God were to speak or to reveal Himself to you, would you be ready to hear it? Or are you going through life so distracted that even the loudest alarm would not wake you? Many people assume God does not speak to them simply because they are spiritually slumbering. They're not listening for God, so they never hear Him. But, for those who are paying attention, God has actually revealed a lot about Himself to us through the Bible.

We know He's our creator (Genesis 1:1) and that His great love for us compelled Him to send His Son to die for us (John 3:16). We know that He is holy and righteous and that those who die without faith in Christ will face eternal separation from Him. (Leviticus 11:44; 2 Peter 3:9; 2 Thessalonians 2:10).

We can read about the many miracles He performed, the greatest of all of them being Christ's resurrection from the dead.

God cares deeply for children, widows, the needy, the homeless, and the desperate. He made a spring of water come from the ground so a single mom and her son would not die in the desert (Genesis 21:18–19). He gave a widow jars of unending flour and oil so she and her son could have food in lean times (1 Kings 17:14). He grew a shady vine to protect his prophet from the sun (Jonah 4:6), gave another young widow a second chance for happiness (Ruth 4:5), raised a young boy to life (2 Kings 4:35–36). He is not silent. He is not distant. He is personal and near and He wants to get *your* focused attention.

"EXTRA" REVELATION?

There is a danger in thinking God is speaking to you when He is not. In fact, many false religions are based on just that kind of mistake. Fourteen hundred years ago, a man named Muhammed believed God had revealed to him new Scripture through the angel Gabriel, and he had his scribes write it down in what would be called The Qur'an. Islam was born. Similarly, in 1830 Joseph Smith published The Book of Mormon, which he claimed was a further revelation from God, and thus founded the Mormon religion. There is a very real danger whenever you deviate from the Bible and claim to have a "further revelation" from God, and it has led to many of the cults and false religions in the world today.

HAVE YOU EVER . . .

had a seriously vivid dream?

So did Joseph, Solomon, Daniel, Peter, Ananias, the king of Egypt, and the wise men from the East.

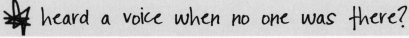

heard a voice when no one was there?

So did Samuel, Elijah, Moses, Gideon, Saul, and the Disciples.

sensed God's presence in nature?

So did Moses, the disciples, Elijah, Jonah, the Egyptians, and Noah.

seen God work miracles when you prayed?

So did Moses, Elijah, Gideon, Peter, Jesus, and millions of others.

had such a strong impression or feeling that you had to act on it?

So did Philip, Peter, Paul, and others.

been visited by an angel?

If so you would be in the company of Abraham, Mary, Joshua, Gideon, and others.

Have you heard God give you direction from a bush that was on fire but didn't burn up? How about from a donkey? Has God written strange writing on your bedroom wall, or communicated to you through lamb's wool, a pillar of fire, or clouds in the sky? It would be pretty safe to assume your answer is no, because there is no record in the Bible of God ever using these methods more than once. The truth is, God used *numerous* different means to get people's attention.

God has spoken to people from the beginning of time, and He is perfectly able to converse with you in a hundred different ways today. The way in which He speaks is not important, but the fact that He *communicates* with you is the key.

This is not to say that *any* unusual experience can be chalked up to God speaking to you. He has given His final authority in the Bible (Revelation 22:18–19; 2 Timothy 3:16), so anything He does communicate will align totally with the Scriptures. If someone claims, "God spoke to me from heaven today and said 'Strip thy neighbor of all he dost have,'" you can be sure that was not a divine command. God will never contradict Himself.

YOUR GUIDE

When Jesus told His disciples He would ask His Father to give them "another Counselor" to be with them forever (John 14:16), the original word He used (translated as "another") didn't mean "one in addition to the other." It meant, "one exactly the same as the one before." So the Spirit of God is the same in nature, character, purpose, and mission as Christ Himself. It makes sense, doesn't it? Jesus, while He was on the earth in human form, was limited to being in one place at one time. But the Christian faith was about to rapidly explode and spread throughout the world. That's why Jesus told His disciples it was good for Him to leave, so that the Holy Spirit (who is not limited by a physical body) could come and guide each of them. The Holy Spirit would take what Jesus wanted His followers to know and declare it to them (John 16:12–15). And He would continue to guide Christians all over the world through to this day.

Take a minute to review some of the many examples from the Bible. In the following verses, <u>underline the</u>

different things that Jesus says the Holy Spirit would do for the people involved.

Mark 13:11: "So when they arrest you and hand you over, don't worry beforehand what you will say. On the contrary, whatever is given to you in that hour—say it. For it isn't you speaking, but the Holy Spirit."

Luke 12:12: "For the Holy Spirit will teach you at that very hour what must be said."

John 14:26: "But the Counselor, the Holy Spirit—the Father will send Him in My name—will teach you all things and remind you of everything I have told you."

John 16:13: "When the Spirit of truth comes, He will guide you into all the truth. For He will not speak on His own, but He will speak whatever He hears. He will also declare to you what is to come."

Now underline the things the Spirit did for people in the first churches:

Acts 20:22–23: "And now I am on my way to Jerusalem, bound in my spirit, not knowing what I will encounter there, except that in town after town the Holy Spirit testifies to me that chains and afflictions are waiting for me."

Acts 16:6: "They went through the region of Phrygia

and Galatia and were prevented by the Holy Spirit from speaking the message in Asia."

Acts 13:4: "Being sent out by the Holy Spirit, they came down to Seleucia, and from there they sailed to Cyprus."

Acts 13:2: "As they were ministering to the Lord and fasting, the Holy Spirit said, 'Set apart for Me Barnabas and Saul for the work I have called them to.'"

Acts 11:12: "Then the Spirit told me to accompany them with no doubts at all. These six brothers accompanied me, and we went into the man's house."

Acts 10:19: "While Peter was thinking about the vision, the Spirit told him, 'Three men are here looking for you.'"

Acts 8:29: "The Spirit told Philip, 'Go and join that chariot.'"

Romans 8:14: "All those led by God's Spirit are God's sons."

1 Corinthians 2:13 "We also speak these things, not in words taught by human wisdom, but in those taught by the Spirit, explaining spiritual things to spiritual people."

1 Corinthians 2:10: "Now God has revealed these things to us by the Spirit, for the Spirit searches everything, even the depths of God."

Did you notice all the action words in these verses? *Reveals, searches, leads, prevents, sends, gives, teaches, guides, testifies.* The Holy Spirit is not a passive observer, but rather God's provision for speaking to His people and actively guiding us as we walk with Him.

PAYING ATTENTION

When I (Tom) was a child, I had a terrible pain in my side. I felt horrible and started vomiting. I was too young to know what was happening, but my mom rushed me to the hospital emergency ward. She had guessed (correctly) that my appendix had ruptured. If she had ignored the physical signs, I would probably have died. I'm so thankful for a mom who paid attention and watched over me.

God wants to get your attention.

He wants to speak to you personally. The way God speaks is always through the Holy Spirit who uses four basic means to communicate with you. The following (several) chapters will take a closer look at each of these. God speaks by the Holy Spirit through
1) the Bible,
2) prayer,
3) circumstances, and
4) the Church to reveal Himself, His purposes, and His ways.

God is God. He can speak to His people however He chooses. That is not our choice. But we do make the decision to watch and listen for Him and to be ready to do what He tells us.

We've said this already, but it's a crucial truth that can't be understated:

If you do not have a relationship with God, then you will not hear Him when He speaks (John 10:3-5).

So what's the most important thing you can do to know God's will? Walk closely with Him. When you do this, your heart will be sensitive to what He is saying.

WALKING WITH GOD

1. What do you think God is saying to you at this time?

2. It is the role of the Holy Spirit to teach you. What do you think He wants you to learn as you read through the Bible?

3. If you do all the talking when you pray, leaving no time for listening, take a moment today to be quiet when you come into God's presence. Allow Him to speak to you.

4. As you take time to read in your Bible this week, read each phrase carefully Ask God to tell you the things you need to know.

5. Before you go to church or Bible study next week, ask God to speak to your heart through the speaker's message. Bring a notebook with you to write down what you think God is saying to you through His servants.

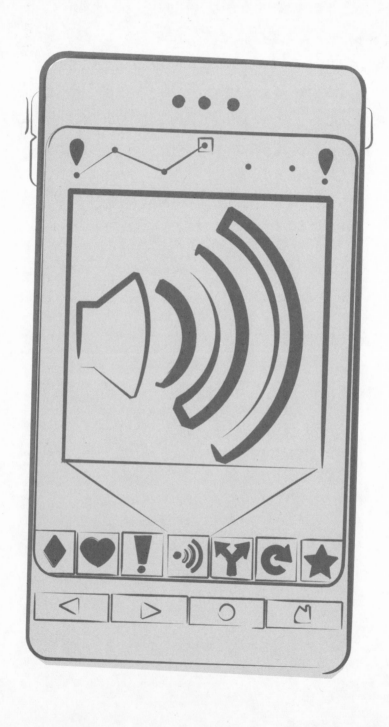

STEP 4 (PART 1): GOD SPEAKS THROUGH HIS WORD

"For the word of God is living and effective and sharper than any double-edged sword, penetrating as far as the separation of soul and spirit, joints and marrow. It is able to judge the ideas and thoughts of the heart."
—Hebrews 4:12

Have you heard the old story about the young man who was looking for direction from God? He decided to try the "open and point" method. He flipped open his Bible to a random spot and laid his finger on a verse.

It happened to be Matthew 27:5. It said: "So he threw the silver into the sanctuary and departed. Then he went and hanged himself."

Not really liking that option, he tried again. This time his finger fell on Judges 9:48, "hurry and do likewise" (NASB).

Third time's the charm. He tried it one more time. He landed on John 13:27: "Therefore Jesus said to him,

INTERESTING FACTS ABOUT THE BIBLE

- 66 books with 40 different authors
- 1,189 chapters; 31,101 verses
- The system of chapters was introduced in A.D. 1238 by Cardinal Hugo de S. Caro and the verse notations were introduced in 1551 by Robertus Stephanus
- Longest name is Mahershalalhashbaz (Isaiah 8:1)
- Longest verse is Esther 8:9 at 78 words
- Shortest verse is John 11:35: "Jesus wept."
- Middle books are Micah and Nahum
- Middle verse is Psalm 118:8
- Middle chapter is Psalm 117
- Shortest chapter (by number of words) is Psalm 117
- Longest chapter is Psalm 119 (176 verses)
- Shortest book (by number of words) is 3 John
- Longest book is Psalms (150 chapters)

'What you do, do quickly'" (NASB).

So much for that method.

When we treat the Bible like a magic book of secrets, or use it to find verses that support what we want to do, we are misusing the Scriptures. We need to remember that when we open God's Word we are not just reading an ordinary book. The Bible is called the Holy Bible because it was inspired by God.[34]

The apostle Paul, in a letter to Timothy (the young pastor he was mentoring), said it this way: "All Scripture is inspired by God and is profitable for teaching, for rebuking, for correcting, for training in righteousness, so that the man of God may be complete, equipped for every good work" (2 Timothy 3:16–17).

---

34. *Inspired* is a translation of a Greek term *theopneustos* that means "God breathed."

WHERE ARE THE ORIGINALS?

You may have asked the question, "Do we have the original manuscripts of the Bible?" The answer is, "No, and that's probably a good thing." If you ever get the chance to go to Israel, you will see how every single place, artifact, or building that can be tied back to the Bible in some way has been turned into a shrine. Huge, ornate churches sit on every place of biblical significance. Also, major wars have been fought for hundreds of years over every holy site in the Middle East. Can you imagine what might happen if the original biblical books were available? What kind of wars between Christians and Muslims would be fought? What kind of greed would drive people to own the copies? What kind of fanaticism or religious hatred would have them destroyed? Instead, this is how God worked it out: We have more than 14,000 copies of the New Testament books alone, which are spread throughout the entire world for all to share. This way, nobody can hoard them all to themselves, but with that many copies to compare and study (which were meticulously copied over the centuries by scribes who devoted their lives to accurately reproducing the text), we can be certain that they faithfully tell us what the originals said. If you still have questions, check out Craig Blomberg's book *The Historical Reliability of the Gospels.*

The Bible is more than just a book written thousands of years ago and is still the best-selling book of all time. It is living and active (Hebrews 4:12 NASB), and it will accomplish God's intentions (Isaiah 55:11). The disciple John wrote, *"In the beginning was the Word, and the Word was with God, and the Word was God. He was with God in the beginning"* (JOHN 1:1–2).

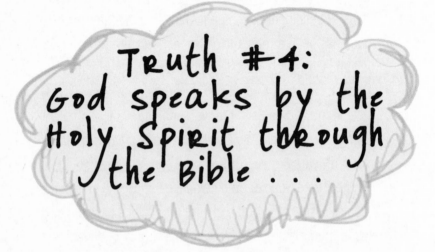

Truth #4:
God speaks by the
Holy Spirit through
the Bible . . .

When we talk about the Word of God, we are not just referring to the printed book but to God Himself, who continues to work His purposes out in the lives of all those who trust in Him. So when you read your Bible, you are interacting with God as He speaks His word to you.[35] Paul spoke about this truth in 1 Thessalonians: *"Here is another reason why we constantly give thanks*

---

35. When Mike and Dan's mom first became a Christian at the age of eighteen, she hadn't quite grasped this truth yet. She was embarrassed that her Bible was so new and looked so "unread." So she took it outside, dropped it on the dusty ground, and started stepping on it to make it look more used. Don't worry; she didn't get struck by lightning! Christians don't worship the physical paper and ink of the Bible, but we *do* believe it contains God's revelation (which means "to uncover what was previously hidden") to us about Himself.

to God: When you received God's word, which you heard from us, you did not accept it as the word of humans but for what it really is-the word of God, which is at work in you who believe" (2:13 ESV)

The primary way God speaks to us today is through His Word. Spending time studying the Scriptures will bring not only head knowledge about spiritual matters, but wisdom and personal guidance so you can know the very best that God has for you. The Bible is literally a life-changing read. Neglecting to read God's Word is rejecting God's chosen means of communicating with you and answering your questions. We are so fortunate in North America to have such easy access to the Bible. What a waste for us to not take advantage of the privilege we have, when so many around the world desperately wish they could have just one page of the Bible to read.

WHAT'S IT WORTH?

Following my high school graduation, I (Dan) spent two weeks on a mission trip to Brazil. Joined by a translator, our team got onto a small boat and ventured far down the Amazon River looking for villages where we would unload medical equipment and minister to the people.

Suddenly there was a rustle in the grass and a splash in the water about a stone's toss from us. Startled, I turned to see what it was. The guide shrugged indifferently, "Oh no worries. Let's keep going. It's just an anaconda."[36]

---

36. Oh sweet mercy, they can *SWIM*!! Must have slipped the guilde's mind the day before when he had Dan and the team jumping in the river.

WILLIAM TYNDALE
[1492–1536]

Tyndale lived in the days when people did not have access to the Bible in English. It was only available in Latin, and only the educated clergy could read it. So the majority of people relied on the clergy to tell them what it said. Tyndale had an argument with a clergyman one day who declared that he would rather be without God's laws than the Pope's. Tyndale was appalled, and he vowed to make it so that the simple boy who drove the plow would one day know more about the Bible than the clergyman. He set out to translate the Bible into English, which was not a popular move. At one point, the bishop of London decided to purchase all the remaining copies of Tyndale's Bible and burn them to keep people from reading them. The merchant, however, was a friend of Tyndale's, who gave him the money from the purchase, allowing Tyndale to print a revised edition—and three times as many.

Tyndale was eventually betrayed and executed. His dying cry was, "God, open the king of England's eyes!" God heard his prayer, and three years later a copy of the English Bible was placed in every church in England. Seventy-five years later, the King James Version was produced, relying heavily on Tyndale's translation.

No worries?? I had worries!

If you've never had the pleasure to meet one, ana-condas are the largest snakes in the world. (They aren't venomous though. They prefer crushing the life out of their victims rather than going the venom route.)

We had just gotten out of the boat when I heard a loud scream from behind me. Aghhh! The snakes are attacking! I spun around in terror. A young village girl, no more than eleven or twelve, was racing down the hill toward me. When she reached me, she placed a small amount of valuables in my hands. With tears in her eyes, she spoke animatedly in her native language.

The translator exchanged several quick words with the young girl. Then he turned to me to explain, "Dan, what this girl has just handed you represents everything her family has. It is their entire life savings. She knows it's not very much, but they hope it's enough to trade you for a Bible."

The look in that girl's eyes will never leave me. She was ready to give away everything she had for the chance to own a Bible. That same trip I met a man whose English Bible was so worn out from reading that it looked like a rag. That man barely spoke English.

These people didn't value the Bible because they thought it was an interesting read or contained some good wisdom. They treasured it above all other things because they knew it was a doorway into the presence of a living God. What is your Bible worth to you?

CLOGGED

 When I (Mike) was a seminary student, I had a bad habit of pouring grease down the kitchen sink. The campus housing authorities had sent out a mass e-mail asking students not to pour grease down their kitchen sinks, but I completely ignored it.

Every time I did it, I had a sinking (pun intended) feeling that it would come back to haunt me. Sure enough, one day as I poured grease down the sink, running water began to rise from the drain. I frantically checked for a blockage, but found nothing; the problem was in the pipes. My roommate and I began vigorously bailing out grimy water with a mopping bucket. You'd think we were going down with the *Titanic*. However, even after we poured Drano down the hole, the clog remained. Our only remaining option was to call campus maintenance. But then I would need to come clean about ignoring the grease rule. . . .

Although I suggested that we could live without a kitchen sink, my roommate turned on me. He called maintenance the next day and then left me alone to confess. As the fix-it man tried to figure out the problem, I managed to dodge most of his probing questions. But once he opened the pipes, all my excuses came flooding out in the form of grease-mixed-with-Drano sludge. It spewed all over the two of us, which prompted the maintenance man to run to my bathroom sink screaming, "My eyes!" I thought he was being a tad dramatic, but the source of the clog was revealed; it looked as though an entire bucket of Crisco had been shoved down the pipe.

"How many times did you pour grease down this sink?" he asked me.

"Well," I shamefully replied, "perhaps once or twice."

CLEAR THE PIPES

Sin in our life is sort of like grease in a sink. (Chances are, you've never thought of it that way!) It's hidden just below the surface so you can't necessarily see it, but it's building up little by little. It is nasty, and it clogs up the entrance to our heart. Eventually evidence starts to surface like the stagnant water in Mike's sink until we finally realize we need to come clean. You see, in order for God's Word to truly speak to us, we have to make sure it gets to our heart. The very best way to have a receptive heart is to pay attention to what we pour into it. The music we listen to, the games we play, the movies we watch, even the places we hang out—all of those can be like heavy globs of grease blocking our access to God.

God once said to His people through the prophet Jeremiah: *"I spoke to you, rising up early and speaking, but you did not hear; and I called you, but you did not answer"* (JEREMIAH 7:13 NKJV). The sin in their hearts caused enough obstruction that they could not hear when God was clearly speaking to them. God will speak to you through the Bible, but you must have a heart that is ready to receive His word.

JUST READ IT

Don't let the weight of sin in your life keep you from opening yourself up to God. We know that sometimes a person feels so much guilt and regret they want to avoid God's Word altogether, rather than dive into it. But the Bible is where your help is. The Scriptures hold the truths that can help you find forgiveness and healing. Pick up your Bible and begin to read, carefully and prayerfully. Don't rush. As you become aware of a specific sin in your life, don't avoid the subject just because it's nasty. Confess it to God and ask Him to forgive you. Ask the Holy Spirit to help you turn away from the sin that has been keeping you from the Father. You will experience a spiritual cleansing that unclogs the pipes to your heart, leaving a clear path for God's Word to speak directly to you. Read the Bible with expectation and anticipation for what God will say to you.

A LOVE STORY

Let's say you find a stack of papers shoved to the corner of your bedroom one day. Would you be excited to find out they were some old math notes from a couple years ago that somehow got misplaced? Would you be like, "Awesome, I can't wait to stay up all night reading these!"? Probably not (unless you are completely sick). But what if you discovered they were letters from someone you cared deeply about? Someone who loved you very much? The Bible is far more than a collection of wise sayings and intriguing stories. It is more than a history of the Israelite people and a sociological study on the nature of humanity. And it is not intended to be a science textbook or an archaeological treasure map. Considered in the above terms, it can seem downright boring.[37]

---

37. Have you ever lost track of time because you were so enthralled by reading the book of Leviticus?

But essentially the Bible is God's expression of love for us. The New Testament writings contain the culmination of the love story, when God provides the ultimate gift to show His love. His Son Jesus Christ suffered to atone for the sin of every person who is seeking to know God. Surely so great a sacrifice wasn't made so that people could learn a bit of history or dabble in psychology.

Read the Bible with the understanding that you're not the audience; you're part of the script. This reality should radically change the way you approach God's Word.

BEDTIME STORIES

In the 2008 film *Bedtime Stories*, Skeeter is called upon to babysit his niece and nephew for several nights. He gets them to bed by telling them fictional stories, which begin by reflecting his frustrations at work. However, strange things begin to happen, and the events of his bedtime stories begin occurring in real life during the day. Suddenly, these stories take on a whole new importance when Skeeter becomes part of the story! He begins to view everything with brand new eyes.

So, what does the Bible actually say?

In the beginning everything was perfect just as God intended it to be. But with the entrance of sin into the world, things went terribly wrong. Ever since sin came on the scene, murder, corruption, deceit, treachery, and violence have permeated the human race.

The Bible says that over and over again, people rejected God; yet He kept drawing them back to Himself with His great love. His people repeatedly cried out to Him for help when they faced the consequences of their sins, and God forgave them and restored them to a rela-

THE SIN CYCLE

REJECTION OF GOD

RESTORATION

TERRIBLE MESS

FORGIVENESS

CRY OUT TO GOD

tionship with Him. And then the next generation came along and repeated the same scenario.

The notable constant from the beginning to the end of the Scriptures is God working to restore the relationship that was lost because of sin. What a tenderhearted God we have that He would not leave us to our own destructive choices. So how do we respond to such love?

LET'S TRY IT

Let's take a look at one passage of Scripture and read it within the context we've been talking about. Turn in the New Testament to the book of Ephesians, chapter 4, verse 29. Here is what it says, "No foul language is to come from your mouth, but only what is good for building up someone in need, so that is gives grace to those who hear."

What is Paul saying? Watch your mouth? Don't curse? Don't gossip? Sure, all those things.

But there is more to it than just not saying some things. He talks about our responsibility to others to help encourage them, to build them up, not tear them down with criticism, name-calling, and negative talk. Paul also talks about giving grace to others. Not based on whether or not they deserve it, but based on our decision to be gracious.

There's a lot of action required from just this one

verse. It means we need to be positive and cheer others up when they're down, help them carry their load if they're overwhelmed or help them have courage if they are afraid. If we know someone's self-esteem is low, it's our job to find positive words that will help them see how worthwhile they are. And according to this verse, that's what God wants our fellow Christians to do for us too.

Do you see the difference between merely reading the Bible as an outsider versus participating in what God wants you to do? It's enormous.

Take a moment or two to think about how just this one verse applies to your life. Have your words been used to build up others lately? Or, have you spoken critically about others, tearing them down, even gossiping about them? If you were to read the above verse one morning and keep it front and center on your mind all day, how would that affect the way you spoke all day? Would other people consider you to be an encourager? Do you need to make a better effort to clean up your language,

THE POWER OF A BOOK

Ray Bradbury's classic novel Fahrenheit 451 describes a dystopian America where all books are burned, and reading is strictly forbidden due to the dangerous ideas reading can produce.

Guy Montag, one of the firemen charged with burning the books, begins to question what's so special about books that people were willing die for them. A former university professor offers him these words:

"The magic is only in what books say, how they stitched the patches of the universe together into one garment for us."

Montag goes on to join with a secret society called the Book People who have memorized entire books including the Bible.

The story is a great reminder that we shouldn't become so focused on the physical book and binding that we forget to let the book's message go to our hearts.

drop your questionable jokes, stop gossiping about others, or being less critical of others?

Isn't it amazing how merely one small passage of Scripture can lead to a complete turnaround in behavior and action? That's because God's Word is alive and powerful, and through the Bible God wants to relate to you personally.

AWAKENED BY LOVE

 I (Tom) once drove to see my brother some eight hundred miles away from where I lived. I decided to bring my two-year-old daughter with me to visit her cousins. It had been a long drive, and it was getting dark. My daughter was asleep in the car seat in the backseat, so I had the radio on very low so not to wake her up. But my eyelids were so heavy, I could not keep them open. I tried everything. I rested one eye, then the other, but they just would not stay up. I shook my head, changed positions, but suddenly my eyelids ganged up on me and slammed shut at the same time. I remember drifting into a nice, warm, comfortable sleep going sixty-five miles an hour. Just then I heard a small voice from the darkness of the backseat say, "Daddy, I love you." My eyes shot open, I corrected my veering car, and only the sheer love of a father for his daughter kept sleep at bay until we arrived safely that night. Words of love have the power to keep you on track, to keep you safe. That's what the Bible contains—powerful words of love.

We hope this chapter has been helpful to you. It's a

life-changing discovery when you comprehend that the Bible is more than just a book. That's why men and women throughout history have given their lives in order that we could have a copy for ourselves to read and interact with the Author. The Bible is God's Word to His people, and it will speak directly to your heart. If you want to know and do the will of God in your life, reading the Bible is where you should begin.

WALKING WITH GOD

1. How often do you read your Bible?

2. What habits could you develop so that you are regularly engaged in God's Word each day?

3. What is your favorite book of the
Bible? What do you like about it? What
book do you relate to the most?

3. As an exercise for growth, go to a book or a passage of Scripture that seems like it doesn't apply to your life at all. What message is God saying through these verses?

4. Is there any way they apply to you as a character in this great story?

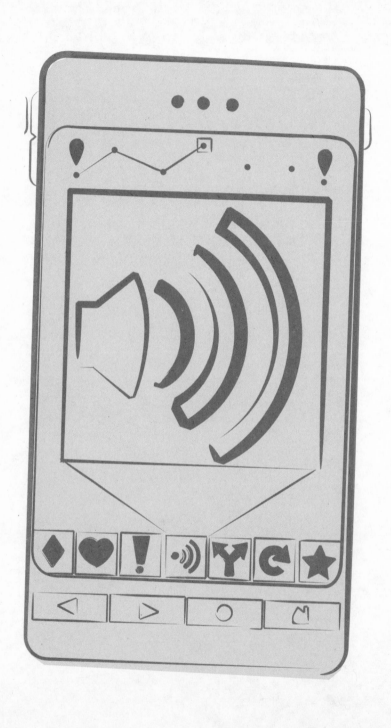

STEP 4 (PART 2): GOD SPEAKS THROUGH PRAYER

"Call to Me and I will answer you and tell you great and incomprehensible things you do not know."
—*JEREMIAH 33:3*

I'LL HAVE THAT "TO GO," PLEASE

 Her eyes inflamed with steely determination, her left eye twitching slightly in anticipation. "This is no drill, soldier," she said through gritted teeth. "This is as real as it gets." Without another word we tightly fastened our seat belts. We both knew what was at stake. It was the calm before the storm; I took a deep breath. *ZOOOM!*

The family minivan screeched out from the garage, sparks flying from the spinning tires. Flinging around in a 180-degree pivot, she kicked it into fourth gear and we were off! Just another day of errands with Mom.

She had been naively deceived into becoming a stay-at-home mom after Mike's birth. He had been so cute! However, two years later marked the end of an era; the age of downtime was over. As I (Dan) charged out of the womb crying and needy, I ushered in the age of stress. She was like the Energizer Bunny, her mammoth to-do lists requiring bookmarks, and on this particular outing she had about thirty-eight stops to make with approximately twelve minutes to make them.

We'd made good progress. Our tires were worn down to the rims. Our feet floated on a pool of accumulated sweat on the floor, and we weren't on speaking terms, but we had made it to page 3 of the list. Around 3:00 p.m. we finally decided on a pit stop at McDonald's drive-thru for lunch. I could see my mother's face redden as the guy in front of us apparently had never navigated through a drive-thru before. Impatiently tapping her fingers, she shot anxious glances at the clock, "Come *on*! Is no one else *ever* in a hurry!?" Finally we pulled up. Without a breath she blurted, "Two-burgers-no-onions-a-coke-and-a-sprite-make-it-quick-buddy!"

"Yes, ma'am. Pay at first window; pick up at second window."

Peeling around to the window, my mother threw money at the worker, "Just-keep-the-change-I-don't-have-time!" My mom then entered into light speed toward the dry cleaners, mumbling about the slowness of "fast" food these days. Nervously I interrupted her, "Um . . . Mom . . . weren't we going to get our food?" My mother realized that after paying she had blown right past the second window without picking up our order.

Isn't that the way we treat our prayers to God sometimes? We put in our request and then dash off to finish the rest of our to-do lists without even sticking around for the answer.

Truth #4: God speaks by the Holy Spirit . . . through prayer.

POOR COMMUNICATION

Few things are as frustrating as poor communication. In an age where worldwide connections are simply a click away, is it any wonder that prayer has largely fallen by the wayside? In reality, prayer is the most accessible tool of communication we have, yet it is also the most misunderstood.

Mike and Dan's mom (bless her heart) tries her best to keep up with communication technology. But it takes her a while to catch on to each innovation. When texting was a brand new concept,[38] she was with our sister Carrie in a shopping mall (a recurring theme in their

---

38. Was there life before texting? She claims there was.

HELPING OURSELVES

Marketdata Enterprises did a study several years ago and found that America had spent eleven billion dollars that year on self-help products (books, CDs, seminars, etc).

In Steve Salerno's book *Sham: How the Self-Help Movement Made America Helpless*, he details the "eighteen-month rule." He found that on average, customers of self-help products have purchased similar products within the last eighteen months.

There is lots of "help" available to cycle through. If one doesn't yield immediate results, we can always move on to the next. Or at least that's what we're told.

God says, "Be *still,* and know that I am God" (Psalm 46:10 NKJV, emphasis mine).

lives). Mike's apartment was nearby, so she thought they should meet up for lunch.

"Carrie, could you text Mike and check about lunch?" she asked. Although she had not yet joined the texting population, she knew it was quicker and more convenient than calling. Carrie obediently typed in a brief message to her brother and started to put the phone in her pocket to await his reply. Immediately, Mom asked, "Well?"

"Well, what?"

"Well, what did he say???"[39]

Carrie had to enlighten her that messaging was fast, but it wasn't instant. One actually had to give the receiver a few seconds to read the message and respond.

We all act impatient sometimes; it's human nature.[40] But maybe it's an even bigger

---

39. Impatience is another recurring theme in our family.

40. Comedian Brian Regan jokes about the outrageousness of having instructions on a Pop-Tart box. He observes that, although it takes less than one minute to toast a Pop-Tart, the box actually provides an even quicker method: microwave for three seconds! He concludes, "Listen, if you need to zap fry your Pop-Tart before you head out the door, you might wanna loosen up your schedule!"

problem because our generation is so used to instant gratification. We aren't used to waiting, at least not the way God wants us to. He promises good results if we will just wait on His timing (Isaiah 40:31). But instead, many of us treat prayer as though we're chatting on Facebook. We casually lift up a prayer of need if the circumstance calls for it and expect His immediate reply. If it doesn't come right away, we grow irritated with God and chat with someone else.

DEAD ZONE

I (Mike) am an impatient person (do you see a family trend here?), and most of my everyday frustrations stem from this problematic trait. One thing that really aggravates me is inconvenience. I thrive in the fast-paced expediency of modern culture. So, when I moved to an apartment complex with terrible cell phone reception, life got a little more difficult.

I had often heard of so-called "dead zones" but had never experienced one. A dead zone can drive a person to madness. One day I found my roommate sitting in the corner, neck stretched into an unnatural position, and his cell phone raised to the sky. "I think I—nope, lost it again," he grumbled. Glancing out the window, I saw my neighbors trying to obtain the same elusive signal. Students wandered the parking lot yelling into their phones, men and women stood on their cars screaming, "Why me?!" to the heavens, and I saw one individual trudging off into the wilderness. (I don't recall ever seeing him again.)

I fared no better than my disgruntled fellow humans. No matter where I stood/sat/leaned/crouched/laid/jumped/crawled in my apartment, I could only grasp reception for a few fleeting minutes. I was down to my last option: patience. I am still in the process of learning this virtue and have been successful in not throwing my phone against the wall, due largely to the fact that I cannot afford another one.

There are days when God seems silent and unreachable. Have you ever felt that way? Sometimes it would be nice if God were just to rip the roof off of our bedroom and loudly proclaim His will for us.[41] However, maybe there is more to prayer than us telling God information. Perhaps prayer is more about changing us and growing closer to God and His will rather than checking off a personal wish list. In fact, how often do we even take time to really listen for an answer to our prayers? It seems like we more often rush in and out of God's presence, expecting Him to speedily work within our busy schedule.

We have discovered that prayer works much better as a two-way conversation rather than a monologue. Have you studied any Shakespeare plays lately? Don't you just love the soliloquies? The poor guy who gets the role of Hamlet has to memorize all those. His one-sided "conversations" are usually either a) a temper fit full of complaints and selfish whining because someone stole the kingdom out from under his nose, or b) a kind of self-therapy session. (Should I have killed my uncle? Yes, I

---

41. The ancient historian Eusebius tells of the emperor Constantine having an experience like this. He was marching with his army when a heavenly sign appeared to him as if coming from the sun. With it was the message In Hoc Signo Vinces or "with this sign, you will conquer." Constantine adopted the symbol (a combination of the Greek letters Chi and Rho) for his army, and claimed the Christian faith as his own.

JOHN "PRAYING" HYDE

John was not known as "Praying Hyde" for no reason. He enjoyed deep communion with God through prayer, and God used his life mightily as a result. Hours spent in prayer meant that Hyde knew exactly what was on God's heart so that he could join Him at work.

In 1908, Hyde sensed that God wanted him to lead one person to faith in Christ every day that year. By the end of the year, 400 people had been saved. The next year, Hyde claimed that God would save two souls a day for a year. He was again proven right when 800 people gave their lives to Christ that year. Finally, in 1910, due to much time spent in prayer, Hyde set the impossible goal of seeing four people saved each day for that year. Amazingly, God did it.

A man like John Hyde could set impossible goals because he was not really the one setting them at all. His close fellowship with God through prayer allowed Him to know the heart of God, and align his life with it. What does God desire to show you through time spent in prayer?

Taken from Wesley L. Duewel, *Heroes of the Holy Life: Biographies of Fully Devoted Followers of Christ.*

THE LORD'S PRAYER

Our Father in heaven,
Your name be honored as
holy.
Your kingdom come.
Your will be done
on earth as it is in heaven.
Give us today our daily
bread.
And forgive us our debts,
as we also have forgiven
our debtors.
And do not bring us into
temptation,
but deliver us from the evil
one.
For Yours is the kingdom
and the power
and the glory forever. Amen.
—*MATTHEW 6:9–13*

should have killed him. But I was too chicken. Why am I such a coward? It's my mother's fault. In fact all women are to blame.) And don't even get him started on Ophelia and whether he should or should not have married her. Our prayers should never resemble a soliloquy or monologue.

So if that's what prayer isn't, let's now focus on what prayer is or should be.

TALKING WITH GOD

Praying is intimidating for many people. After all, it means talking with our Creator. Lots of people feel embarrassed to pray out loud because they don't know what to say. When you're not used to talking to somebody, it can be awkward at first.[42] But the more you get to know them, the easier and more natural it becomes.

God is our heavenly Father. God is your heavenly Father. He wants you to approach Him as a child

---

42. Let's hope it's never as awkward as when Mike was a teenager and saw a friend at the mall with several of her girlfriends. Mike was set to transfer to their high school that fall, and when he spoke up to introduce himself, his voice cracked like a broken radio! Luckily, the more you talk to people, the more comfortable you get—even after bad first impressions!

would go to a loving parent (John 16:26; Luke 11:13; 18:16).

What would that look like? Well, first and highly important, it would include trust and respect, but also a boldness in knowing that the Father loves you deeply and wants to hear from you. The assumption is also that the parent is the one who guides the child and helps solve the problems. Even intervenes when necessary (Luke 21:12–15). And listens when your heart has been broken. And dries the tears.

Let's get even more specific. When you pray, ask your heavenly Father what is on His heart and mind and allow Him to direct your thoughts. Here are several principles about how to pray and corresponding verses from the Bible to help you :

1. Find a quiet place.

Matthew 6:6: "But when you pray, go into your private room, shut your door, and pray to your Father who is in secret. And your Father who sees in secret will reward you."

A quiet place is best but can sometimes be hard to find. Mike and Dan's uncle Jim grew up as the only brother of seven sisters in an extremely small house with just one bathroom. There were not many places to escape, but Jim liked to get a stack of peanut butter sandwiches and a good book, and lock himself in their one bathroom to soak in the tub for hours. There, his only distraction was the intermittent pounding on the door from a desperate sister, threatening all manner of cruel payback. But he learned to tune that out. If you're creative like Jim, you'll find an out-of-the-way place too.

✳2. Remember God knows your heart.

Matthew 6:7–8: "When you pray, don't babble like the idolaters, since they imagine they'll be heard for their many words. Don't be like them, because your Father knows the things you need before you ask Him."

You're not going to tell God anything He doesn't already know, so what He is looking for in your prayers is not information, but your heart. He wants you to tell Him your concerns, your thoughts, your fears, your joys, and your dreams.

Don't try to sound fancy. Think about what you're praying and be genuine, whether you are praying in public or in private.[43] God isn't so much looking at the words you say as He is the condition of your heart. God knows what is in your heart regardless of what your words say anyway. "These people honor Me with their lips, but their heart is far from Me" (Matthew 15:8).

✳3. Pray expecting God to answer.

Mark 11:24 "Therefore I tell you, all the things you pray and ask for—believe that you have received them, and you will have them."

You can tell how much people believe in prayer by how they respond after they pray. We've been a part of youth outreach events where the group met together early and prayed, "God fill this place with people tonight," and then only set up half the chairs. The Bible says if you

---

43. Maybe we're nitpicking, but here are two possible clues that a person is not thinking about what they are praying: A) When people say "Lord" 96 times in a 30-second prayer. ("Lord" is a title; it's not punctuation.) B) When people pray before eating and end it by asking God to "bless this food to the nourishment of our bodies." Um, you just prayed that over a heaping plate of nachos. Perhaps people just assume that if God can turn water into wine, He can turn nachos into broccoli.

don't believe God will answer your prayers, there is really not much point in you praying in the first place. God rewards our faith and satisfies the hearts of those who believe. Several times Jesus healed people and said, "Let it be done for you according to your faith!" (Matthew 9:29; 15:28; Luke 5:20; Mark 2:5; 5:34; 10:52).

When Mike and Dan were growing up, they attended church with a middle-aged British woman named Christine. She believed in prayer. This was evident one time when she had a package she needed to deliver to our house.

We had just moved to a new neighborhood, and she didn't know our address or phone number. So she just started driving in the general direction of where she knew the neighborhood was. As she drove, she prayed.

She drove past three community entrances until she got to the fourth. Turning into this one, she followed the winding road all the way until she almost reached the end. As she rounded the last corner, she spotted us as we were walking into the garage after a game of driveway basketball. She pulled in and delivered her package to our door.

When we discovered how she had found us, we were all astounded, but we shouldn't have been. That's the way Christine lived her whole life. She prayed for everyone, and she prayed about everything.

4. Pray for yourself.

Matthew 26:41 "Stay awake and pray, so that you won't enter into temptation. The spirit is willing, but the flesh is weak."

It is okay to pray for yourself. When Jesus spoke the above words, He was about to face death on a cross. If we were in that position, we would have told the disciples, "Pray for me!" And yet Jesus told them to pray for themselves. Even the model prayer that Jesus gave His people (see The Lord's Prayer on p. 148) asks to give us our daily bread, forgive our sins, keep us from temptation, and protect us from evil.

We need God to intervene in our lives, and prayer helps to get us on the same page with Him about what He wants for our lives.[44] In fact, the more time we spend in prayer, the more time God has (if we're listening) to align our hearts with His.

5. Pray for others.

Matthew 5:44: "But I tell you, love your enemies and pray for those who persecute you."

Praying for others is a way we can show love for them. There is no greater support and encouragement people can have than when others are lifting them up in prayer to God. We like to tell people, "I'll pray for you," meaning we'll pray later. And that's fine, as long as we remember. But sometimes you have an opportunity to pray for someone at that moment. And even better yet, if the person is okay with it, offer to pray with that person at that moment.

---

44. Dan was once in an awkward situation where a girl was "aggressively pursuing" him as her chosen BF. As a last ditch move, she called him and declared that God had told her they were to be together. Dan was so terrified it might be true that he didn't pray for weeks! Thankfully, she had "misheard" God! Nevertheless, when you pray that God aligns you to His heart, you must be prepared for what He answers.

6. Pray with others.

Matthew 18:19: "Again, I assure you: If two of you on earth agree about any matter that you pray for, it will be done for you by My Father in heaven."

God loves to see His children working together. Prayer can unite a church as they all seek God's heart together. A girl in Mike's young adult group has suffered for years from a mysterious illness. One Sunday evening the whole congregation gathered to pray over her. She was not healed that evening, but God did a powerfully unifying work among the believers who sought His heart together. The sense of unity has been noticeably stronger to this day. Also, God has been working in this young lady's life, and He continues to use her sweet spirit to encourage many others. She knows her church family loves her, and we continue to pray for her regularly. God does not just have a will for us individually, but also as a church body.

7. Ask God to help you know what to pray for.

Romans 8:26: "In the same way the Spirit also joins to help in our weakness, because we do not know what to pray for as we should, but the Spirit Himself intercedes for us with unspoken groanings."

The great thing about prayer is that even rookies who don't yet know how to pray can do it. Sometimes even longtime Christians find themselves in a situation where it isn't clear what to say or what to even ask for. But God is present in our circumstances, and the Bible says the Holy Spirit takes over for us.

Have you ever been in this place where you have no idea what to say to God? That's okay, because God knows your heart. Sometimes silent prayers are the most powerful.

Because prayer is probably the most misunderstood part of the Christian life, we want to be sure and look at both sides of the coin. So before we move on to the next chapter, let's briefly recap several things prayer is *not*.

WHAT PRAYER IS NOT

Prayer is not bringing your shopping list to God for Him to answer.

Prayer is not telling God what to do.

Prayer is not our right; it is our privilege.

Prayer is not getting what we want done it is God getting what He wants done.

Prayer is not a duty, a habit, or a religious ritual it is the natural outflow of a personal relationship with God.

Prayer is not for showing off, for giving announcements to the congregation, for making people feel guilty, or for manipulating others.

We hope this chapter has given you a better understanding of the tremendous privilege we have to go before God in prayer. Just remember, communication is a two-way exercise. If you ever find yourself just bringing a Christmas list of requests to God, you'll know it's time to stop and listen. What is it that God wants to reveal to you through prayer? Don't let impatience keep you from waiting on God. We've found that when we start praying for His will to be done, not ours, that's when we start to hear back from God. He is looking for a heart that longs to hear from Him, not just tell Him things. Times of prayer can be some of the sweetest times you spend with God.

Take some time right now to pray and ask God to reveal to you what is on His heart. You may be surprised at what He says to you when you take the time to listen.

WALKING WITH GOD

1. How often do you pray? Do you mostly pray by yourself or with others?

2. When you pray, do you usually do most of the talking? Are your prayers mostly filled with requests?

3. Our prayers can often reveal how selfish we are. How many of your prayers are about you and how many are for others?

4. What has God revealed to you recently through prayer? Has He given you direction in your prayer times?

STEP 4 (PART 3): GOD SPEAKS THROUGH CIRCUMSTANCES

"God sent me ahead of you to establish you as a remnant within the land and to keep you alive by a great deliverance. Therefore it was not you who sent me here, but God."—Joseph, GENESIS 45:7–8

THE DATE THAT NEVER WAS

I (Dan) had it all planned out. It would be perfect. I stood and confidently marched out of the war room, leaving maps and a compass on the cluttered table.

It was time:

The Target: A cute girl named Sarah
The Objective: Have her fall madly in love with me
Code Name: Operation First Date

I dressed in my best clothes,[45] and shoved the piles of garbage in my car beneath the front seat (and therefore, forever out of existence). As Sarah crawled into the passenger seat, I tossed my hand to my forehead, exclaiming, "Did my heart love till now? Forswear it, sight! For I ne'er saw true beauty till this night!"[46] Sarah politely turned up the radio.

We arrived at the movie theater and I, being chivalrous, purchased her movie ticket.[47] During the "dramatic" moments of the chick flick, I sniffled and wiped away invisible tears, offering her an alluring teaser to my more "sensitive side."

After the movie, we shared a romantic dinner at Manchu Wok in the food court. I even ordered us extra spring rolls, just to let her know she was worth it. The time came for the grand crescendo. I launched into telling riveting tales of my ten most memorable hockey victories (in chronological order). She laughed! She cried! She . . . mostly looked back and forth people-watching (obviously overwhelmed by Victory #4: The Miraculous Comeback of '05).

Finally, when our enchanting evening came to an end, I reluctantly dropped her off at the door with the parting words: "Good night, good night! Parting is such sweet sorrow! That I shall say good night till it be morrow!"[48] Mission Accomplished.

---

45. My most recently washed sweater and jeans with the least amount of holes.
46. From Shakespeare's *Romeo and Juliet,* of course!
47. With my trusty 2-for-1 coupon.
48. That's right, more Shakespeare. She's mine now. . . .

Well, okay, it took six months for her to become my girlfriend, but the sprouting seeds of love had obviously been planted that night. A month later, while reminiscing about our relationship, I asked, "Remember that first date: the movie and the food court? Wasn't that a magical evening?"

Sarah paused for an awkward moment, confusion on her face. "Oh . . . I didn't realize that was a date."

Truth #4: God speaks by the Holy Spirit . . . through circumstances.

YOUR WORLDVIEW

Two people can look at the same scenario in completely different ways. You no doubt have experienced this phenomenon as well:

You go to the theater and absolutely hate the film,[49] yet afterward you overhear other people raving about it as the greatest movie in the history of cinema.

Seventh grade was a nightmare. You hated every second of it, but the buddy who sat in the desk next to you all year talks about it as "the glory days."

---

49. *Transformers 2*, we're looking at *you!*

After a youth rally at your church, you are stoked and excited for God, but on the way home your best friend groans about how dull and boring it was.

How is it possible for two people to see things so differently? The reason is because everything you do or think is filtered through your life experiences. It is unavoidable. We each have a "worldview." It's like a lens through which we interpret everything that happens to us (good or bad). It colors the way *we think*, the things *we value*, and, ultimately, the way *we live*.

Your worldview is largely shaped by your experiences, and your experiences are then interpreted through your worldview. It's a cycle that we are continually going through. This circular process is how we develop our understanding of the world around us. The more you talk with people (especially from other cultures), the more you will notice how different our worldviews can be.

WHERE'S THE TOILET? [YES, ANOTHER SEWER STORY BY TOM]

I (Tom) was told everything would be much different in a developing country, and they were right. In a Senegal village I found grass huts, dirt floors, and a well in the center of town where people heaved on long ropes to bring up a bucket of water. I could accept that, and it was actually kind of fun. So when I went to a developed country overseas, I expected a lot of normal things. Beijing, China, is a huge city, very modern with lots of electronics, people, cars—you name it. Luckily, after reaching my quota of fried rice, I found a KFC restaurant. I had been looking for a bathroom all day and was quite happy to finally find one. I excused myself from my friends and hurried to find the "facilities." I closed the door, and—where's the toilet? It was gone!

In fact whoever stole the commode had also

AN EMERALD CITY

In L. Frank Baum's novel *The Wonderful Wizard of Oz,* Dorothy and her band of peculiar companions follow a yellow brick road to reach the majestic Emerald City.

At the front gate everyone is given mandatory green sunglasses to block the "brightness of the city."

They later remove their sunglasses and make a shocking discovery: The city is "no more [green] than in any other city." It is only the glasses that color their world green.

taken the toilet paper. *There must be pretty desperate people around here,* I thought. Then I noticed the hole in the floor and a bucket of water sitting beside it. It didn't take me long to do the math, and when I did, I realized I was about to have an experience I would *not* want to talk about when I got home.

So why is a worldview important? Because through it you will interpret the experiences that happen to you. Just think of how different we interpret thunderstorms from those who lived many years ago. The reason why Norse mythology developed the character of Thor, the god of thunder, was to try and understand the great mysteries of weather. Today we know more about static electricity in clouds and the science of weather. However, there is always a danger in interpreting our experiences in the wrong way. . . .

BEHIND DOOR NUMBER ONE . . .

A couple of years ago, I (Mike) volunteered to chaperone a trip for my church's youth group over New Year's. It turns out, my friend Jeff was arriving in town late New Year's Eve and needed a place to crash, so to avoid hotel costs I offered to leave him the spare key to my place. I told him where to find the hidden key and said to just let himself in.

Jeff arrived at my apartment around four in the morning. He was groggy and exhausted from hours of driving. He found my key and tried the door. It didn't work. He assumed he had the wrong door. Turning around, he saw steps leading up to another door.

Desperate for sleep he figured he would give that one a try. The key worked.

He went in and trudged up a small staircase to the bedroom. As he fumbled for the light switch he noticed something in the dimness. Wow. Good news! It was a king-sized bed. He flipped on the light. Wow. Bad news! There was a couple sleeping in the king-sized bed—he was in the wrong place!

You see, I lived in a small apartment attached to a larger house. They were completely separate living spaces with no access to each other, but apparently one key worked in both locks. My aunt and uncle lived in the house.

Awakened by the intruder, my aunt jolted up and shook her husband awake. Blurry-eyed and confused, he demanded that Jeff identify himself as he scrambled for the gun he kept by the bed. My trigger-happy uncle was from Texas where you shoot first and ask questions later. Luckily Jeff was able to blurt out my name before my uncle pumped him full of lead.

A COMMON MISCONCEPTION

There is a common misconception that says, "If the door opens, it must be right!" Many Christians operate on the assumption that just because there seems to be an "open door," then it must certainly be God's will for us to walk through it. Perhaps it's an opportunity for a part-time job that opens up, or the girl we like suddenly starts talking to us, or the coach of the basketball team asks us to try out, or that college promptly mailing an acceptance letter.

One reason we love to seize an open door is simply because it's there. We want to act now, and this is our chance. We talked about being impatient in earlier chapters and told you some lighthearted stories about the trouble it has gotten some of us into. But make no mistake: being in too much of a hurry to listen to God is a serious problem. It's never a good idea to rush impulsively through a door unless you know it's the right one for you (ask Jeff!).

The Old Testament tells of one occasion (1 Samuel 24) where David had the perfect opportunity to kill his tormentor King Saul and take his rightful place as king. David was God's choice for king and he knew it, but King Saul was doing everything he could to prevent that from happening. Then another day David and his men happened upon Saul, who was sound asleep (1 Samuel 26). This definitely looked like an "open door" if there ever were one. But David didn't do it. Why? He knew there would be a proper time and place where God Himself would exalt him and give him the throne. And that's what did happen eventually. That's why David could write these words in Psalm 40:1: "I waited patiently for the LORD, and He turned to me and heard my cry for help."

Don't assume God's will is always the most readily available oppor-

PIPES

There's an old computer game that helped Mike and Dan survive countless computer classes at school. It was called Pipes.

You would start with an unfinished pipe system. Then the vile green liquid would start flowing. The player was required to construct new pipes (Tetris-style) before the liquid reached the end and spilled.

When God directs your life, He doesn't run ahead of you frantically opening and closing doors to force you down one path. His plans are much more than that. The entire system is already in place.

HORTON HEARS A WHO!

The classic Dr. Seuss story tells of the Whos of Whoville as they go about their daily lives. Things change when the mayor of Whoville meets Horton —a giant elephant.

Horton informs the mayor that in fact, all of Whoville is located on one microscopic speck and is part of a much bigger world.

Horton dedicates his time to protecting the speck from the dangers of the much larger world as the Whos carry on as normal, oblivious to the world outside their speck. Most of the citizens of Whoville don't know that a greater world even exists outside of their own.

Many Christians are like the Whos. They have such a small worldview that they never fully realize that God is at work and has greater plans outside of the speck that they are familiar with.

tunity. Or that an obstacle means you are not where you should be. Overcoming that obstacle may be God's will all along! Be patient, prayerful, and wise, and God will lead you in the way He wants you to go. The closer your walk with God, the easier it will be to know step-by-step where He is leading you.

A BIBLICAL LENS

Our experiences must be interpreted in light of Scripture. It is by filtering the world through a biblical lens that you can rightly interpret your experiences.[50] If your experience contradicts what God has said in the Bible, trust the Bible over your experience, because God will never go against His Word.

"I believe in christianity as I believe that the sun has risen, not only because I see it, but because by it I see everything else."

—C. S. Lewis

---

50. This means that, as a Christian, everything should be interpreted through your Christian faith. Nancy Pearcey says, "'Thinking Christianly' means understanding that Christianity gives the truth about the whole of reality, a perspective for interpreting every subject matter." (Nancy Pearcey, *Total Truth: Liberating Christianity from Its Cultural Captivity* [Wheaton: Crossway, 2005], 34)

We are especially vulnerable to misinterpreting our circumstances when we are hurting or going through a crisis. That's when many believers conclude that God must not love them, because surely a God of love would never let such terrible things happen, right? We cannot determine who God is simply based on our experiences because we can't see the whole picture. Many times, once we are on the other side of a painful experience, only then can we clearly see how God was involved and active the whole time, walking with us through it and shaping us to look more like Jesus. It is especially during painful times that we must believe what God has told us about Himself in His word. Cling to promises such as, *"I will never leave you or forsake you"* (HEBREWS 13:5).

In order to properly interpret your experiences, you must spend time with God in prayer and in His Word. The more you know Him, the more you will recognize how He speaks through your experiences. When this is happening properly, it will become very obvious to you when God is speaking.

There's a story about some good friends of ours that illustrates what we mean when we say God's Holy Spirit speaks through circumstances, along with Bible study, prayer, and through other Christians. (The next chapter will delve more deeply into the way God speaks through other believers.)

It's important to note that our friends were patient to make sure they were hearing from God and did not just rush off into something extreme. But when you know that God is speaking to you, do not delay your obedience.

MOVING TO ORLANDO

Griffin and Jennifer were living the American dream. An attractive couple in their mid-thirties with two terrific kids, a son and a daughter, they lived in the state where they both grew up, so both had family nearby. They were rooted there; their children were happy, and they were deeply involved in a growing church plant. Griffin, a highly talented musician (and former rock star), was enjoying leading the music at their church. Even in a bad economy, they both had good jobs.

Jennifer says that every time God is about to ask her to make a major adjustment in her life, He prepares her in advance. A year or so ago, she sensed that a decision was coming that would push her far from her comfort zone.

She went about her life and her job and stayed busy in her church, but she began to watch for what God might have in mind for her. She began to meet more and more people from Florida. Each time she did, a strange vision would play out in her mind where her family was living there. "Wouldn't it be crazy," she thought, "if after meeting all these people moving to South Carolina from Florida, we switched places with them?"

Meanwhile, Griffin was working almost eighty hours a week in several jobs and sleeping four to five hours each night. He usually slept like a log, but one week he woke at exactly 4:44 a.m. three different times. This was unusual, and it wasn't until a few days later that it occurred to him that the answer might be found in his Bible.

During his morning Bible study time, he looked up every book of the Bible that had a 4:44. The three

STEP 4 (PART 3): GOD SPEAKS THROUGH CIRCUMSTANCES

occurrences in the Old Testament yielded no results (Numbers 4:44, Deuteronomy 4:44, 2 Kings 4:44). Then he turned to the New Testament. Luke 4:44 read, "And he kept on preaching in the synagogues of Judea" (NIV). John 4:44 said, "Now Jesus himself had pointed out that a prophet has no honor in his own country" (NIV). He called Jennifer and said, "We're moving to Judea!" They both laughed, but now each had a sense that God was preparing them for something.

A couple weeks passed. Then Griffin got a text from a man he hadn't heard from in seven years. The man lived in Orlando, Florida, and was offering Griffin a possible job, as well as a position leading worship in a new church plant. Griffin had been looking for a new job for the last four months, and on three occasions he thought for sure he had it, only to be turned down at the last second each time. And now a man in Florida was offering him two jobs at the same time! When he called Jennifer to tell her about it, he half expected her to say no, but instead she said, "Call him!" The problem was, there were several hurdles standing in the way of moving.

Both of their kids were in school until May. Jennifer was scheduled to take a mission trip to Africa at the end of the month. It was a terrible time to sell their house, and they knew exactly four adults in all of Orlando. But they trusted God would work it out if He really wanted them to relocate. Then Griffin got a "pocket call" from his cousin's phone—one of the four people he knew in Orlando. Her two-year-old daughter had accidentally called his number. Then Jennifer's dad randomly told Griffin he was thinking of buying tickets to Orlando to help Jennifer's mom get over her fear of flying because the flights there were so cheap. They noticed a series of TV commercials with the tag line "Orlando is calling."

Griffin talked to his pastor and asked him to pray about their situation. The next day a call came: could Griffin start the Florida job in mid-May? That gave them less than four months to sell their house.

During the time leading up to this moment, Jennifer had been personally dealing with the difficult possibility of leaving her parents and her sister. They had never lived more than twenty minutes apart their entire lives. One day she went to work at the hospital where she was employed. They have a policy that no employee is to be left alone with a patient. During lunch, it happened that Jennifer was the only one available to do an MRI, so her boss called one of the secretaries to join her. The secretary arrived and burst into tears. Jennifer (a little weirded out) asked if the lady was okay, and the woman responded, "Now I *have* to tell you! But you're going to think I'm crazy!"

Jennifer smiled: Too late for that.

The secretary was a Christian but was not very outspoken. During her prayer time that morning she had sensed God wanted her to specifically tell Jennifer to "Go." She knew nothing about Jennifer's potential plans, so she had no idea what this strange instruction meant. The lady told God, "I will only do this if you open up the opportunity to talk to her alone." And here she was a few hours later with a message from God at the right time. By this time Jennifer was weeping too.

The house was put on the market, and Jennifer was ready to head to Africa. While boarding the plane, she received a call from her husband. They had just sold their house for cash to a pastor and his wife without any inspection! The pastor's wife had told Griffin to call Jennifer right away so that she wouldn't worry while on her way to Africa.

By the end of May, Griffin and Jennifer were Floridians. God has blessed them and expanded their lives and their ministry. Mike's college group has since taken a mission trip to help them at their church plant and witnessed God's obvious activity in that place. Do you see how God guided this family through each circumstance they found themselves in? They were sensitive to the activity of God in their lives, and as they filtered their circumstances and experiences through their Christian worldview, God led them step-by-step to exactly where He desired them to be.

When you are walking closely with God, He will use Scripture, prayer, the church, and experiences to guide you to where He wants you to be. What an exciting way to live! It will not always be easy, or immediate, but it is always worth it. Is this what you desire? Has this been your experience? It can be.

WALKING WITH GOD

1. Have you fallen prey to the "Open/ Closed Door" theology? Has there been a time when a door looked closed, but you waited and God opened it?

2. Many of those involved in New Age philosophies today base their religion completely on self-experience. What are the dangers of this?

3. How can you make sure your experiences
are really God's way of speaking to you?

4. Where in the Bible did God use a person's experiences to lead and guide them?

STEP 4 (PART 4): GOD SPEAKS THROUGH THE CHURCH

"And let us be concerned about one another in order to promote love and good works, not staying away from our worship meetings, as some habitually do, but encouraging each other, and all the more as you see the day drawing near."—HEBREWS 10:24–25

DON'T LOOK DOWN!

I (Mike) have always loved climbing. When I was a kid, I used to scamper up trees, I never lost a game of Grounders on the playground, and I even slept on the top bunk. So when I recently had the opportunity to go rock climbing, my answer was an enthusiastic, "Yes!"

Sure, I was a little less flexible than I was in my youth, my love for Arby's hadn't done me any favors, and my new exercise regime remains perpetually on last year's New Year's resolution list, but how hard could it be?

Our crew trekked through the beautiful wilderness of North Carolina until we arrived at our destination—a sheer cliff wall dozens of feet above us. *Okay,* I thought, *so we're skipping Beginner and going straight to Intermediate. I can handle this. . . .*

My turn arrived, and I began my ascent up the rock. I could feel the strength seep from my limbs as I moved up the mountain one painful inch at a time, until I reached The Spot. The Spot was a section of the rock that nobody had successfully passed, and I was no different.

I clung to the rock like Steven Tyler is clinging to his youth. I did not have an ounce of strength left in me. My limbs were shaking, and I was too weak to pull myself up any further. Sweat poured down my face as I bowed my head against the wall. And then I saw it: a giant spider. I hate spiders.

With nowhere to run, I felt panic overtake me. My worst nightmare was slowly crawling on eight scrawny legs toward my exhausted limbs. It felt like a scene out of Indiana Jones. Cue the close-up of my sweaty-yet-handsome face. But no, this was real.

Desperate to escape, I remembered that a sturdy rope held me securely from the clip attached to my waist. With renewed confidence, I channeled all my energy into pulling up on the rope and unleashed a kick to make Chuck Norris envious. The spider went flying to what I hope was his sorry demise, and I breathed a sigh of relief as I hung suspended from the rope waiting for my buddies to come and help me down. I didn't make it to the top that day, but I chalk it up as a success, just the same.

CREATED FOR COMMUNITY

Ecclesiastes 4:9–10 says, "Two are better than one because they have a good reward for their efforts. For if either falls, his companion can lift him up; but pity the one who falls without another to lift him up."

There have always been people who shunned the idea of "organized religion" so they chose not to be part of a church. According to their view, a person's spiritual journey is a private matter, between them and God, so they see participation in a Christian community as optional.

The Bible teaches something different. The Christian walk was never meant to be taken alone. In fact, Jesus said that the two greatest commandments are to love

THE AVENGERS

This 2012 movie brings together a team of superheroes, including Captain America, Thor, Iron Man, The Hulk, Hawkeye, and Black Widow. They are each so different that conflict within the group is inevitable, but they unite to fight a common enemy. When the evil Loki comes on the scene, he is too much for any one hero to handle. However, by their combined strength and their diverse abilities, The Avengers accomplish together what they could never do individually.

God and love people (Matthew 22:34–40). But how can you really love people if you are not connected to them? How can you practice your spiritual gifts to build up the church if you're not part of a church (Romans 12:4–6)? If the Bible uses the body of Christ as a metaphor for what the church looks like (1 Corinthians 12:12–14), and we are divided and not connected to each other, what does that say about Christ? Is Christ Himself divided? The truth is, we were created to be in community with each other. We are the body of Christ as believers, but we often choose to step back and try going it alone.

We've noticed that those Christians who are experiencing a vibrant walk with God are the ones plugged in to a church community. Why? Because we were designed to live out the Christian life together (1 Corinthians 12:26; Romans 12:5).

WHY IS IT SO IMPORTANT?

Being a part of the body of Christ holds many advantages, for you as an individual Christian as well as for the body itself. Please note: This will not be a discourse on church membership, denomination, or affiliation. Rather, we want to focus on how God uses the body of Christ to accomplish His purposes.

One obvious advantage of having a church family is that it includes many different people from all walks of life with diverse talents and skills. You can learn from the innocence of a child or the wisdom of a senior adult. You have people who have been where you are and successfully navigated through those challenges and you have people coming behind you that can benefit from your journey. When you pull away from your local

church, you limit one of the greatest ways the Holy
Spirit speaks into a Christian's life.

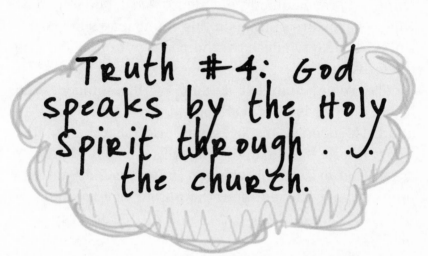

Truth #4: God speaks by the Holy Spirit through . . . the church.

CONFIRMATION THROUGH OTHERS

A young man was struggling to know what God's will
was for his life. He had just completed law school, but
had a deep conviction that God wanted him to go into
full-time Christian ministry rather than practice law.
But it wasn't an easy decision. For one thing, his parents had paid a *lot* of money to put him through law
school. There were other circumstances as well that
weighed on him. He desperately needed confirmation
before taking such a radical step.

One Sunday during the altar call at his church, he
knelt at the front to beseech direction from God. Henry
Blackaby was in the same service. Many people were

kneeling at the front to pray that morning, but Henry's eyes were drawn to that young man in particular. Henry sensed God moving him to go and join him in prayer, so he slipped out of his seat, knelt down beside the younger man, and prayed quietly, but aloud. "Lord, I do not know what it is you are putting on this young man's heart, but I pray that he would have the courage to obey you no matter what."

The young man felt a hand on his shoulder and heard the words of prayer spoken directly into his situation. He opened his eyes and was shocked to find Henry there beside him. Tearfully, he told Henry, "I asked God to confirm whether He was calling me into ministry, and He sent you, the author of *Experiencing God: Knowing and Doing the Will of God* to pray with me."

The Holy Spirit will use members of your church to help you gain wisdom. It's so easy to get wrapped up in our own life that we sometimes need an outside party to speak wisdom to us. This is especially important when we're caught in the trap of sin, even though that's the least likely time we want to hear it. In 2 Samuel 12, we read about God using the prophet Nathan to help King David repent of his sin. David showed no intention of ever confessing what he had done (which included adultery and murder) or repenting of it. Nathan was God's prophet sent to bring a word of correction to David. It takes courage to confront a king, but by cleverly using a hypothetical story, Nathan helped David grasp the enormity of the sins he had committed. As for David, he realized that God loved him too much to let him continue in his path to self-destruction, and David repented. The Bible even refers to David as "a man after God's own heart." Sometimes God will use a Christian brother or sister to step in and bring us to our senses when we are blinded by our own sin. It's not fun, but it's worth the awkwardness if it gets us back on the right path.

If you are living with sin in your life, you cannot hear clearly from God and walk in His will. You must first deal with that sin before you can begin to follow God's will. Be thankful if you have a friend or family member who loves you enough to risk angering you by confronting your sin. That's just one of the ways God uses the church to speak to His children.

GOD REVEALS HIS LOVE THROUGH THE CHURCH

Mike's church throws a banquet each year for widows and widowers. Most of these people are elderly, and they struggle with loneliness as well as financial need. This banquet provides a way for the church to show the

THE GRINCH

In this Christmas classic, the Grinch attempts to ruin everyone's Christmas by stealing all the gifts. The truth is, he doesn't really understand what Christmas is all about. In the live-action adaptation of this Dr. Seuss tale, the Whos (especially Cindy Lou) spend the whole movie preaching to the Grinch about Christmas. But you know what finally gets through to him? When he sees them all join hands and sing, without any gifts or presents at all. Witnessing their joy as a community is what breaks through to him and changes his heart.

love of Christ, and God has used it to speak powerfully into the lives of those who attend.

As this year's event approached, the pastor had a special idea. God laid it on his heart to do something unusual. Each guest was given an envelope as they walked in the doors, with the instructions not to open it until the appointed time. After the meal, the announcement was made that the envelopes could now be opened. The room was filled with the sound of tearing paper, followed by audible gasps. Inside each envelope was a letter from the pastor—and a crisp one-hundred-dollar bill. (Aren't they always crisp? They're so seldom used.) One dear widow began to weep, and she shared her story with the others at her table. That morning she had collected all the money she had, which was a modest six dollars. She used five dollars to put gas in her car so that she could drive to church (this was a Sunday morning), and she had sacrificially placed her remaining dollar in the offering plate. She didn't know what she was going to do but trusted that God would meet her needs if she trusted Him. Now, just a few hours later, she had received a hundred dollars! One of the other women at her table was so moved by her story that she gave her hundred-dollar bill to the woman as well.

How did God use the church in this woman's life? She came to experience the provision and love of God in a tangible way. Numerous other guests at that banquet shared about their own situation as well. For some, it wasn't even about the money. It was just knowing that they were loved and cared for. In fact, many shared their intentions about how they were going to pass along the blessing. Most of the people at that event had walked with God for many years. What a joy it was to see their faith grow even stronger as they experienced the love and provision of God through the church.

NONBELIEVERS NEED THE CHURCH TOO

You may see how Christians and members of your congregation are blessed and strengthened through the church. It's God's provision for support during hard times, it's one of the ways He gives direction, and it's a channel through which He brings conviction when we are blind to our own sin. But being part of a church isn't just for the mutual benefit of the congregation, although that's certainly an important role.

The Great Commission is a huge assignment that cannot be achieved by individuals doing their own thing. God will use Christians as they unite together to impact an unbelieving world. In fact, bringing people to Jesus is God's will for your life (2 Corinthians 5:20). This mission is best accomplished when we live in love and unity and the world can see what the Christian life really looks like (John 13:35; 2 Corinthians 5:18).

The Bible says God created us to need one another. He's the One who established the local church (Ephesians 1:22; Ephesians 5:23; Colossians 1:18), and He chooses to work through the church to reach nonbelievers and to teach His followers. If Christians are watchful and obedient, they will see God at work in their fellow church members' lives, and they can be a great source

IMPACTING OTHERS

In the fourth season of FOX's sci-fi series *Fringe*, one of the main characters, Peter Bishop, is abruptly removed from time.

When he finally returns from limbo, he finds himself in a world where he has never existed.

The show raises an interesting question: How would those around you be different without your influence in their life? Would there be a radical change? Or would anyone notice? God's plan for your life always involves other people. Christianity is intended to be personal, but that does not mean it's supposed to be private.

of encouragement. Also, sometimes God calls on us to help other Christians deal with their sin and find forgiveness and restoration with the Father.

God speaks by His Holy Spirit in several ways: through the Bible, through prayer, through circumstances, and through His people.

So far, we have presented the ways in which God directly communicates with us and the ways that He provides guidance for our lives through others. We've touched on several ways we can respond so the Father will use us to work in the lives of others. Now we want to take it a step deeper and talk in more detail about what our response should look like when we receive a clear word from God. Don't let the title of the next chapter (which includes the word *crisis*) deter you from moving along with us to that next truth. We're getting into the most exciting stuff right now.

WALKING WITH GOD

1. Are you actually involved in a church or just attending one? If you are not involved in a church, will you ask God right now to lead you to one that can help encourage you in your walk with Him?

2. Have you been hurt by the church in the past? This is one of the biggest reasons why people distance themselves from the church. Unfortunately, even Christians aren't perfect, and they will mess up. But what might it cost you not to be involved in a church?

3. Can you truly live as an obedient
Christian without being plugged in to a
local church community? Why or why not?

4. What are some of the ways (mentioned in this chapter or other ways you think of) that God might use the church to speak into your life?

5

GOD'S INVITATION LEADS TO A CRISIS OF BELIEF

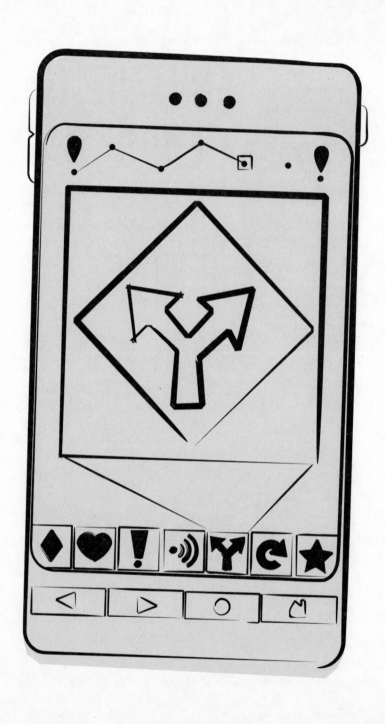

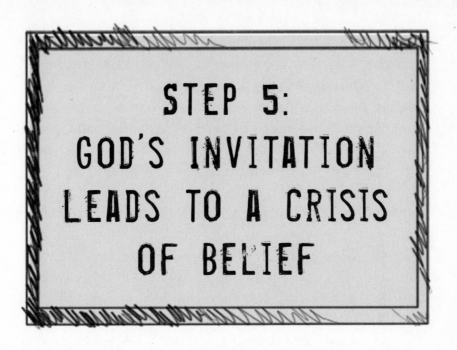

STEP 5: GOD'S INVITATION LEADS TO A CRISIS OF BELIEF

"Now without faith it is impossible to please God, for the one who draws near to Him must believe that He exists and rewards those who seek Him."—HEBREWS 11:6

THIS HAD BETTER BE STRONG VELCRO!

I (Mike) don't like to think of myself as a daredevil. I'm no Evel Knievel,[51] but I have eaten some adventurous foods. (What can I say? My sister likes to cook.) However, when the opportunity presented itself to bungee jump, something inside me was stirred.

---

51. He was a stuntman who did crazy, dangerous things.

Dan and I had traveled to Athens with a group of college students to volunteer for two weeks at a refugee center. While most of our time was spent meeting and helping people at the center, we still had a couple days to experience the sites of Greece. We rented a bus, met up with a local missionary friend, and took a mini road trip to see ancient Corinth. About two hours from our destination we made a rest stop at the famous Corinthian Canal. Although the canal itself is impressive, what caught my eye was a small run-down building off to the side with a sign written in smeared red letters: "Bungee Jumping." Before I could stop myself, I said three words that still haunt me to this day:

"I'd do it."

What was I thinking?!

But then the clouds parted, and a light shone from the heavens and behold a sign which read "CLOSED" (cue angelic chorus). I breathed a sigh of relief. Looks like I wouldn't need to back up my boasting. Unfortunately, our scheming missionary friend called the owners and convinced them to come in and let us jump. I watched in horror as my brother and three of my friends plummeted into the depths of the Corinthian Canal, attached to a cord held by . . . Velcro!? Attempting to look brave I crawled to the ledge. It started to rain.

"No one will push you," the jumpmaster said. I had a choice, to jump or not to jump.

"God, I'll see you soon." I jumped.

At least I wanted to. My legs became like Jell-O, so I kind of just fell forward. My arms flailed like a dancing jellyfish. I was halfway down before I had time to scream. And when I did scream, people began looking around to see where Mariah Carey was performing.

I'll always remember that experience. What a rush! I had never experienced such fear, but I had also never known such excitement.

REVEALING MOMENTS

Have you had times like that? We all experience events that force a choice. And the choice we make reveals what we really believe.

As you seek to follow God's purposes for your life, you will inevitably be thrust into some situations that call for a yes or no. Either you trust God despite your fear and take that the next step—or you don't. Your choice will determine whether or not you experience the fullness of God's plans for you or if you miss out on what could have been. This brings us to a crucial step:

> **Truth #5:** God's invitation for you to work with Him always leads you to a crisis of belief that requires faith and action.

THE GREAT BLONDIN

Jean-François Gravelet (a.k.a. "The Great Blondin") was the first man to walk across Niagara Falls on a tightrope. He did it June 30, 1859.

A great crowd gathered to watch Blondin balance 160 feet above the falls. They cheered wildly as he performed remarkable feats, including pushing a stove into the middle with a wheelbarrow and cooking an omelette!

Blondin asked the crowd if they believed he could push a person across in the wheelbarrow. They exclaimed, "Yes! You are the greatest tightrope walker in the world!" But when he asked who would volunteer, the crowd went silent. No one was willing to risk their life to back up their words.

On another occasion, Blondin wowed the audience by carrying a man across Niagara Falls on his back. Who was this man? Harry Colcord, Blondin's manager. Colcord knew Blondin, and he had every confidence that he would reach the other side safely.

When you know God personally, you know that you can trust Him, even in the most frightening circumstances.

CRISIS VERSUS CRISIS OF BELIEF

Before we go any further, we need to clarify what is meant by a "crisis of belief."

Over the course of a lifetime, you will deal with many crises. We all know people who seem to live in a perpetual state of crisis. By definition, a crisis is a critical situation requiring a difficult decision to be made. So as you can imagine, a decision for one person (like what to wear to school) can seem like a crisis, but for someone else the question of wardrobe is a nonissue.

For the purposes of this book, we refer to a "crisis of belief" in the same manner Henry Blackaby used it in the original *Experiencing God* study. A crisis of belief always has to do with your relationship with God.

EXAMPLES OF A CRISIS:

* You get fired from a job.

* Your grandfather dies unexpectedly.

* Your twenty-year-old car makes its final joyride.

* You get dumped by your boyfriend or girlfriend.

* You get to class and realize you forgot to study for the test.

EXAMPLES OF A CRISIS OF BELIEF:

* God is prompting you to go on a mission trip to Africa, but you are afraid of flying on an airplane.

* God asks you to join a ministry that reaches out to different ethnic groups, but you don't speak their language.

* You sense that God wants you to start a Bible study at your school, which means you will have to take a public stand for your faith.

* You know God wants you to befriend a person who is being picked on at school, but you are reluctant to get involved.

* God calls you to the ministry, but you're terrified of public speaking.

Do you see the difference? You can handle a regular crisis by either fixing the problem or enduring it. But a crisis of belief makes you reevaluate your relationship with God. It's one thing to claim you believe something. It is completely different when you back it up with your actions.

MOSES

What do you think went through Moses' mind as he looked out at the vast Red Sea, knowing that legions of Pharaoh's chariots were bearing down on him, and that the entire nation of Israel was following his lead in their hope to escape slavery? That is a crisis of belief in mammoth proportions. It looked like God had led Moses and his followers directly to a dead end. What Moses did next would show what he really believed about God's promise to deliver the people from their Egyptian oppressors.

Moses put his faith into action, and God came through. This wasn't the first time he trusted God in what looked like a no-win situation. God had been faithful every other time. When Moses stretched out his hand over the sea, God parted it with a strong east wind (Exodus 14:21). Moses was then able to lead the Israelites across the sea on dry land. With mighty walls of water roaring on their left and right, every step they took down the middle was a literal step of faith.

The reason many people don't see God move in amazing ways is because they come to a crisis of belief and they turn away. How about you? Do you really believe God can do miracles in your own life? God does not reward unbelief. A crisis of belief is that pivotal moment when you know what God is asking you to do and you either step out or you don't. Those who believe will experience God in ways that others never will.

Have you ever wondered why God chose to deliver the Israelites out of Egypt in such spectacular fashion? Wasn't there an easier way? Wasn't it cruel to put Moses through that high level of stress? According to Exodus

14:18, God said: "The Egyptians will know that I am Yahweh when I receive glory through Pharaoh, his chariots, and his horsemen." Do you think there was any question who was behind that great miracle? Do you think anybody credited Moses with a really big magic trick? When you read through the Bible, there is an ongoing motif: the larger the task, the more ordinary the person God selects to accomplish it. God easily could have looked over all of Israel and chosen the flashiest politician to provide a rational plan. But who would have received the credit? Instead, God chose a stuttering sheep-herder with a murderous past and sent him on the most impossible route. The result: God spoke loud and clear and no one could question who it was.

WHAT DO YOU REALLY BELIEVE?

Katie was sixteen and felt utterly hopeless and alone. A serious eating disorder had landed her in the hospital. The days were long and dull. She was only allowed to walk (or do any exercise) for a very short time every day. This restriction was necessary because she could not afford to burn any excess calories. Her weight had dropped to a potentially fatal low, and every effort was being made to keep it from dipping even lower. In the brief time out of her ward, she happened upon a small room—it was a chapel. She peeked inside curiously. The instant she did, she felt a strange sensation, something she could not ever remember experiencing before. It was peace.

Katie found herself repeatedly drawn to that small chapel. When she was finally released from the hospital,

LOAVES AND FISHES SUNDAY

The day was September 30. There was a hushed anticipation as the congregation of Bow Valley Baptist Church (Mike and Dan's home church) awaited the announcement.

The church had grown steadily and had outgrown the current sanctuary. Guests were turning away, unable to find seating. After praying, God gave the church definitive instructions.

They were to build a new building. But they first needed to pay off the $450,000 still owed on the current one. Furthermore, they were not to ask for any outside help or do any fund-raising . . . and they were to raise the money in only one offering!

Church attendance averaged 300 people including children, students, and guests. These were middle income people—it was not First Baptist Beverly Hills!

The day came, and the offering was taken. Children emptied the pennies from their piggy banks, teenagers sold their CDs, adults sacrificed their savings. Late that afternoon the congregation met at the church for the final count. A picnic had been planned to celebrate. Our pastor stepped to the podium and shared the news: they had raised exactly $450,000.

Not only that, but by the end of the month the regular weekly offering was the highest total they had ever had. God had asked them to step out in faith—and He didn't let them down.

she attended a local church to try and find out why. Several weeks later Katie accepted Christ. She had never felt such joy and freedom.

But then came the crisis of belief: She had been raised as a Muslim in a Muslim home. Her father was not at all in favor of her choice to become a Christian. He gave her an ultimatum: give up her newfound faith or find a new place to live.

Back at the hospital she had been drawn to God's love and comforted by Him. But to follow God any further meant she would be rejected by her own family and left without a place to live. It was a high price.

Katie had to ask herself: what did she really believe about God? Was it worth the price? Could He really be trusted to provide for her, or would she be all alone to deal with the fallout from following Him? That night Katie stepped out in faith. Over the next few years God not only provided for her physical needs, He has led her on an exciting journey ever since. Was it costly? Yes. But was it worth it? She would tell you, "Absolutely."

GOD-SIZED OR MAN-SIZED?

It was called Big Red. People spoke of it in hushed, frightened whispers. Every time you heard its rattling WHOOSH you knew Big Red had just claimed more victims.

Flashback to our childhood: Once a year Mike and I (Dan) would go with our family to West Edmonton Mall (at the time, the largest mall in the world). Our favorite part was the immense indoor amusement park. We would head straight over to the kiddie section and laugh gleefully as we soared at a blazing two miles per hour on the swing ride. We would throw our hands up as the choo-choo train inched along the tracks. But our favorite was the yellow roller coaster.

Our father with his six-foot-two frame was less than enthused. That he could walk the entire track in three strides of his long legs and find steeper "drops" on a two-by-four plank didn't seem to thrill him. His eyes would wander over to the other end of the amusement park, to . . .

The Mindbender—the largest indoor, triple-loop roller coaster in the world. The colossal monstrosity is colored a dark, sinister crimson (legend says it had originally been gray). The coaster climbs all the way to the ceiling before dropping into a straight 140-foot plunge with a deafening ROAR! Just before hitting the bottom, it swerves in a majestic grand loop. When it first opened, some people were actually killed, but the bugs had been worked out since then.[52] There is a walkway that passes right through the final loop.[53]

Every year Dad would lead us onto that walkway and ask the same question: "Are you boys ready?"

To which we would respond, "No thank you. We choose life."

Year after year my dad would cram himself into the yellow roller coaster until that fateful day came when another family joined us on our trip. They had two boys our age—and they were eager to ride. Gulp.

The line was silent, the riders shuffling forward like cattle being led to the slaughterhouse. After a short delay for "minor mechanical difficulties" we were led

---

52. At least, that's what they *told* us.
53. Our father used to instruct us to hold out our hands for loose change.

into the carts. My knuckles turned white as I grasped the railing and with a loud cranking noise, the coaster climbed higher, and higher, and higher. It stopped at the top—and rolled into the drop of death.

The only sound louder than the coaster that day was the piercing, high-pitched shrieks from Mike. The day we conquered Big Red was the last day we ever rode the yellow roller coaster. How could we ever go back after the adrenaline rush we had just experienced?

PUT IT IN INK

On the day before the 2010-11 NBA basketball season was to begin, the Dallas Mavericks held a team-building event. A tattoo artist was brought in to offer his services.

That's when shooting guard Jason Terry did the unthinkable: he had the NBA championship trophy inked onto his right bicep.

The catch? The Mavericks had never won a single championship in their thirty-year history.

Eight months later Terry stood in center court raising the Larry O'Brien trophy for the world champion Dallas Mavericks.

Terry had full faith in his team and his actions showed it.

When it comes to a relationship with God, some people are forever content to settle for less, when God has so much more for them. Like those two roller coasters, God has something much bigger and better He wants us to experience. But it may mean getting over our fears. Is God asking you to step out of your comfort zone and join Him in accomplishing His work? If so, then you may be standing at a crisis of belief. What you do next will show what you really believe about God. We hope and pray that your next step will be one of obedience to whatever it is God is leading you to do.

God's plans are always larger than what you or I could possibly imagine. Experiencing God always happens on the other side of obedience. Each crisis of belief you come to lands you at a fork in the road. You can choose to obey God or not. Your decision will show what you truly believe about God. The world doesn't need to see Christians doing good things for God; they need to see God doing impossible things through Christians. This only happens when we have faith. There is a big difference between having faith and living by faith. Which one describes your life?

WALKING WITH GOD

1. Describe a crisis of belief you have experienced in your life. What have you done in the past month that required faith?

2. Has there been anything God has asked of you that you have refused to do out of fear of failure or lack of confidence?

3. What would God have to do in your life to show you He is worth trusting?

4. Each time you move past your fear by faith, God rewards you and blesses you. What kinds of rewards do you think God gives His people?

6 ADJUSTMENTS

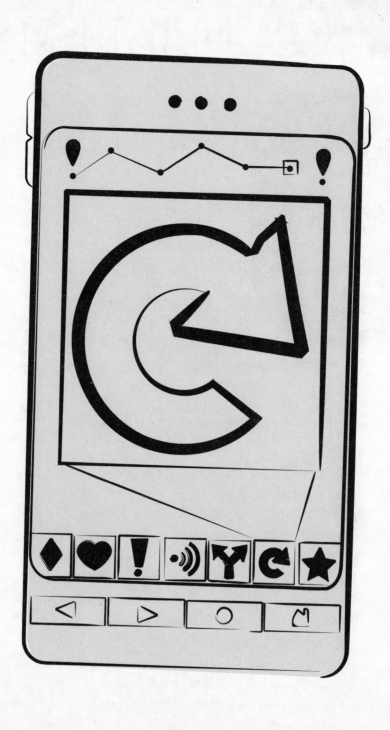

STEP 6:
ADJUSTMENTS

"If anyone wants to come with Me, he must deny himself, take up his cross daily, and follow Me. For whoever wants to save his life will lose it, but whoever loses his life because of Me will save it."—LUKE 9:23–24

CHIPPING AWAY

It was mockingly called "the Giant." An ugly, oversized stone block, deteriorated and faded, sat abandoned in an insignificant courtyard in Italy. It was a hapless end to an ambitious project that had begun with such zeal.

In 1466, the esteemed Italian sculptor Agostino di Duccio was commissioned to turn the expensive stone into the centerpiece of a series of statues. Before long, however, Duccio abandoned the project. The work remained untouched for ten years until Antonio Rossellino was hired to finish the job. Yet, after a while he too walked away, unable to conceive how anything good could come from such a mess. For twenty-five long years the botched project sat untouched.

Finally, one more desperate attempt was made. A twenty-six-year-old Italian artist was signed on to complete the task. His contract described the eyesore as being "badly roughed out." For two years the young artist would chisel piece after piece from that rock until at long last, almost forty years after it was initiated, the sculpture was completed. Michelangelo had transformed an embarrassing monstrosity into the statue of *David*—arguably the greatest, most revered sculpture in human history.

MAKING ADJUSTMENTS

Christians have been bought at a great price. While we were still blemished and stained ugly by sin, Christ paid the highest price—His own life—for our souls.

But that's not all. God originally created us to be a magnificent replica of His own image. But the ravages of sin deformed us, and our numerous imperfections were left on display for all to see. There seemed to be no hope that we would ever be the reflection of God's glory that was our original purpose. But God, the great Sculptor, redeemed us and began the process of perfecting us.

You may be thinking, *This analogy doesn't apply to me because I'm nowhere near perfection.* But God is not like the first two disheartened sculptors; He doesn't walk away in frustration. God always completes what He starts. He will keep chipping away at your sin and smoothing your character until you see Him face-to-face. That's what His Word promises: "He who started a good work in you will carry it on to completion until the day of Christ Jesus" (Philippians 1:6).

C. S. LEWIS DESCRIBES IT LIKE THIS:

Imagine yourself as a living house. God comes in to rebuild that house. At first, perhaps, you can understand what He is doing. He is getting the drains right and stopping the leaks in the roof and so on. You knew that those jobs needed doing and so you are not surprised. But presently He starts knocking the house about in a way that hurts abominably and does not seem to make any sense. What on earth is He up to? The explanation is that He is building quite a different house from the one you thought of. Throwing out a new wing here, putting on an extra floor there, running up towers, making courtyards. You thought you were being made into a decent little cottage: but He is building a palace. He intends to come and live in it Himself.

C. S. Lewis, Mere Christianity

TRUTH #6:
You must make
major adjustments
in your life to join
God in what He
is doing.

THE MOST IMPORTANT ADJUSTMENT

Have you seen the Christian bumper sticker that
declares "God is my copilot"? That is one of the most
common misunderstandings of what it means to be a
Christian. God did not create us, redeem us, and pursue
a personal relationship with us just so He could ride
shotgun while we cruise along in pursuit of our goals.
The imagery is all wrong in that statement.

If you have considered God to be like a Robin to your
Batman or a Chewbacca to your Han Solo, that's the
first adjustment you must make in order to know His
will, join Him in His work, and experience Him.

There is only one driver behind the wheel.[54] It's either you or God. Until you release your death grip on the steering wheel, you will not be able to join God in all He is doing. God's will is not something we can add into our life. Rather, our life must adjust to fit into the will of God.

NEEDLES AND REFLECTIONS

I (Mike) always hated needles; they made me queasy. In fact, when I was a kid, I would actually pass out after a vaccination. In September of 2003 when I was eighteen, I found myself in one of the worst places I can think of: the hospital. I had visited my local doctor about some health issues, and he hastily sent me to the hospital for "tests." (Is there ever a good connotation for that word?)

Waiting in the emergency ward gave me many reasons to be miserable. From the unknown state of my health, to the groaning man behind the mystery curtain beside me, to the backless dress they made me wear, things were not going so well. I was attached to numerous machines. But then two pretty nurses entered the room, and all thoughts of my previous gloom disappeared instantly. That is, until I saw the IV needle.

As one of the nurses reached for my arm and slowly brought her weapon to bear on it, she asked:

"You aren't afraid of needles are you?"

I glanced at the object in her hand; it resembled a tool of medieval warfare.

---

54. Unless you're married . . .

"Of course not," I lied, "I want to stay well hydrated. What's the holdup? Let's get this show on the road."

Both nurses started to giggle, but it was not the "you-are-so-brave-and-rugged-you-make-me-nervous" kind of giggle I might have hoped for. Between fits of chortling, they told me what was so funny.

"You can't lie while you're hooked up to a heart monitor." The machinery beside my bed was displaying my heartbeat, which was about a hundred beats per second. Busted.

"LORD, LORD!"

Many times our words don't reflect what our hearts reveal to be true. But God sees our hearts, which are eventually reflected in our actions. It doesn't matter what we claim about who is in control of our lives. Many people proclaim that they are Christians, but their actions totally contradict their words. In reality, they have no intention of submitting their own will to God. They just want a holy bodyguard to have their back as they go about their daily life. That's called "hypocrisy," and it rightfully confuses a watching world.

The proclamation "Lord!" is heard loudest when broadcast through actions. In the Roman Empire it was believed that the emperors were gods. Citizens were required to acknowledge, "Caesar is Lord." In fact, when Christians refused to call him by this title, they were actually called atheists. Many faced persecution or death for refusing to give Caesar this title, which they reserved for Jesus alone. The title "Lord" represented full authority and required full submission to that authority.

Alexander the Great was once sailing when a strong wind blew the diadem off his head.[55] This distinctive headpiece landed in the reeds, so a soldier swam out to get it. To keep it dry the soldier bound it around his head and swam back to present it to Alexander. He received a reward, but then was flogged (some scholars believe he was actually executed) for "wearing" the royal headpiece.

Obviously, the title of Lord was not taken lightly in ancient culture! How do you think those people would react to the flippant way we use the word today? Even Christians sometimes use the term more like a punctuation mark: "Lord God, I pray, Lord, that, Lord, Your will be done, Lord, and Lord, please be with us today, Lord. Amen."

Perhaps it was the same casual use of the word that led Jesus to chasten: "Why do you call Me 'Lord, Lord,' and don't do the things I say?" (Luke 6:46). Actions speak louder than words. If you truly consider Jesus to be your Lord—and not your copilot, bodyguard, or sidekick—the way you speak and the way you act will show it.

---

55. A diadem was an ornate headband similar to a crown. It denoted royalty or special status.

"You can't go with God and stay where you are."
—Henry Blackaby

LIFE ADJUSTMENTS

Only when we have settled the question of control and acknowledged that Jesus is the rightful Lord of our lives can we actively participate in God's work. God can and does accomplish His plans through whomever He chooses. Even nonbelievers have unknowingly been used by God. But there's a big difference between an active versus a passive participant. That difference is what experiencing God is all about.

God's plans are mysterious and enormous, and they may look nothing like what our own agenda would. That's the exciting part!

Let's turn our attention to the adjustments God might require of us as we move onto His agenda. These adjustments come in all shapes and sizes. The Bible is full of examples of God working wonders through ordinary people. But each of them was called on to step out in faith.

* Abraham had to move his family to a new country to follow God. (Genesis 12:1-8)

* Noah had to alter the way he spent his days (for many years) in order to build the ark. (Genesis 6)

* The disciples had to change their career paths and leave their business. (Matthew 4:18-22)

* Esther had to put her comfort (and her life) on the line to help her people. (Esther 4:14)

* Zacchaeus had to do a 180 on his attitude toward money (Luke 19:8)

* Gideon had to agree to unconventional (an understatement!) battle plans to defeat the Midianites. (Judges 7)

* Mary the mother of Jesus and her fiance Joseph had to sacrifice their reputation. (Matthew 1:19)

* Paul had to abandon his entire theology (Acts 9:1-19)

These are only a few biblical examples of ordinary people whose lives were turned completely around as they accepted God's assignment for them. There are hundreds more in the Scriptures, and we can read about thousands more than that in records of church history. Not one of them would find it easy, but they would all testify that it was worth it. Many of them gave up their lives to prove it.

The common denominator is that all of them were required to move from their agenda onto God's agenda. The truth is, we don't think God-like thoughts. That's why we need Him to guide us. And when He shows us where He is at work and invites us to join Him there, we must revise the course on which we were previously headed.

WHAT ABOUT US?

The adjustments God asks you to make could include any number of factors, but here are a few areas that often need adjustments when God is at work.

Ambitions

The only thing better than Ryan's mullet was his skills at the electric guitar. He dreamed of being a big-time rock star. His band began playing gigs in local bars and clubs, and they were starting to make a name for themselves. However, the musician's lifestyle can be grueling. His family and his Christian faith were starting to take second place to his passion of music. He decided to take a break for a while and agreed to only come back if there was a chance at a record deal.

Not long after this decision, Ryan got a call from an

LITTLE ADJUSTMENTS GO A LONG WAY LITERALLY

Nobody expected much from outfielder Jose Bautista when he was drafted late in the twentieth round of the 2000 MLB draft.

He did little to prove otherwise, as he labored for three whole years in the minors before getting his chance.

But after a series of being cut and traded, the only record he set was by playing for a mind-blowing five different teams in a single year.

Over the next three years, Bautista did little to impress and was finally sent back down to the minor leagues. His career as a professional was seemingly over.

Only one team, the Toronto Blue Jays, decided to take one last shot on the almost thirty-year-old journeyman.

The new hitting coach suggested a few mechanical changes in his swinging stance. Bautista agreed to give it a try. Opposing pitchers wished he hadn't.

After hitting only eighty-six home runs in his first six years, Bautista would crush ninety-seven over the next two seasons alone! He led the league both times.

The willingness to make a few minor adjustments transformed Bautista from an unwanted, washed up benchwarmer to the most feared home-run hitter on the planet.

old bandmate. They had been asked to play a gig where a record producer would be in attendance. This was the chance they had all been waiting for. After the show, the producer singled out Ryan from the rest of the band. "Ryan," he said, "we'd like to work with you, if you're interested." All his childhood dreams were laid out before him, but it called for a tough decision. Continue to sacrifice his faith and his family, or walk away from his dream? Ryan did not sign the contract. He yielded his will into God's hands, for whatever He may ask of him.

Ryan is in his late forties now. God has rewarded his faithfulness. Ryan, his wife, and their two daughters (both talented musicians) travel full-time, playing at churches, conferences, rodeos, block parties, and whatever else God asks them to do. Whereas he once stood to lose his family, Ryan now leads marriage retreats along with his wife, and they enjoy the privilege of glorifying God along with their daughters. Is their life an easy one? Not at all. They put in long days. Ryan is not wealthy and famous, as he might have been. But God had plans all along for Ryan and his wife and their daughters, and Ryan had to decide which direction to take. Would he serve God or fulfill his personal ambition? Thankfully, he chose the former.

Habits

Lynn drank coffee by the gallon. She claims she had exchanged her milk bottle for a coffee mug. One early morning she was enjoying a cup of joe when she heard from God. She knew it was Him, and she sensed He was asking her what she would sacrifice for Him. She decided to show her devotion to God by giving up something she thought she could not live without—coffee.

It was difficult, but she made it through the entire next year without even a sip of java. When she visited her doctor for a routine physical, he asked her to come back in for another checkup and some X-rays. When the doctor asked her if she was a coffee drinker, she told him she had given it up.

It was discovered that Lynn had an aggressive form of breast cancer. The doctors had noticed some tiny lumps, but this is not uncommon in women who drink heavy amounts of coffee so they dismissed them. But when Lynn told them she had given up coffee, they went back for another look. The lumps were cancer. This early detection saved Lynn's life.

God knows your future and the plans He has for you. He does not ask you to adjust your life for no reason. Even small changes you make today will dramatically impact your future.

Relationships

 I (Mike) see all kinds of people who walk through the doors of the cafe ministry I lead at my church. Sometimes, they can be pretty rough characters! On one occasion, a young man, Robert, had recently moved to the area and started visiting our group. He was coming out of the gang lifestyle. He told me stories that made the hairs of my arms stand on end! It all hit home for him when he walked out of his house one day, carrying his two-year-old daughter. Some of his "friends" were waiting and jumped him as soon as he stepped outside. His daughter fell to the ground, and his fellow gang mem-

bers beat him up and stole his wallet. He decided right then that he needed a change of scenery.

Robert had moved many miles, and God had brought him to our doorstep. He expressed his desire to find a new life and find God. I gave him the same advice I have given to many other people: You will rise or fall to the level of the people you put around your life. What he needed was a new crowd. He agreed, and he aligned his life alongside our group of guys who committed to walk with him.

One year later . . . I was sitting at a table in our cafe with a young man who was telling me his story. He had recently moved from New Orleans and had become involved with a rough crowd. Now he was desperately trying to get his life on the right track but didn't know how. As we were talking, Robert pulled up a chair, and I sat back and watched as Robert (now a changed man) gave this young gangbanger the same advice that I had given to him a year ago. I could only smile as I saw the results of well-made adjustments. Sometimes the best thing you can do in your life is change the people you hang out with. Like I told Robert, if you want to go with God, get around other people who are following Him.

"I was ashamed to be less scandalous than my friends, whom I heard bragging about their disgusting exploits; and the more disgusting the episodes were, the more they bragged about them. So I did the same things they did, not simply for the pleasure of doing them, but mostly for the praise I hoped to get."

—Saint Augustine, Confessions

Stuff

The Bible relates an occasion in Mark 10:17–22 when a successful young man came up to Jesus, and asked him a big question. This guy had many possessions, but there was one thing he wanted to make sure he had: eternal life. He asked Jesus what he needed to do in order to obtain this. Jesus gave him a disheartening answer: Sell everything you own and come follow Me. This was an adjustment the young man was unwilling to make. As a result, he never got to experience the wonders Jesus could have done through his life. He kept all of his wealth but missed out on something far more valuable. Here is the most tragic part of that story: Jesus kept on going. He didn't stand there and beg and plead for the young man to change his mind. Although Jesus was disappointed in the man's decision, He continued on with the work of the Father.

Would Jesus ever ask you to give anything up? Would you be willing to do it? There is an old saying that goes, "The more possessions you own, the more possessions own you." In a culture that celebrates excess of material things, what might God ask you to give up in order to follow Him?

God is the Lord of all creation. We are not. He does not exist to help navigate us to where we want to go. He is the one who sees the future and who sees into the human heart. Therefore, if we are to experience a close and personal walk with Him, we are the ones who need to do the adjusting.

The most important adjustment is acknowledging Him as Lord of our life. Other adjustments may involve giving up a habit, maybe even changing our future goals, adjusting where we spend our time and who we spend it with, and loosening our grip on material things. Whatever the adjustments are, God is the One who will let you know. The wisest choice you can make is to do what He asks. Then you will experience Him in new dimensions. That's what the next and final step is all about.

WALKING WITH GOD

1. Can you recall a time when you knew God was leading you to do something that you would not normally do? Did you do it? What happened? If you didn't do it, what do you think might have happened?

2. Jot down the headings: ambitions, habits, relationships, possessions. Under each one, list anything that might be keeping you from following Christ. What adjustments could you make so you can go where God is leading?

3. You should always have three types of relationships in your life at any one time: 1) someone who is mentoring you, usually an older, wiser person, 2) someone who is walking with you, a peer in the same stage of life, and 3) someone you are investing in, maybe from the younger generation coming behind you. Do you have these three relationships in your life? If not, think of someone who could possibly fulfill those relationships.

7

YOU COME TO KNOW GOD BY EXPERIENCE AS YOU OBEY HIM, AND HE ACCOMPLISHES HIS WORK THROUGH YOU.

STEP 7:
YOU COME TO KNOW GOD BY EXPERIENCE AS YOU OBEY HIM, AND HE ACCOMPLISHES HIS WORK THROUGH YOU.

"You are My friends if you do what I command you."
—*JOHN 15:14*

YOUR TURN TO DRIVE

My (Tom) son Matt is a confident kid. Captain of the high school soccer team, captain of the senior basketball team, and he even enjoys public speaking—something most people would rather have a needle stuck in their eye than do.

So when it came to learning how to drive, he felt he was not going to have any problem. He had driven hundreds of cars on the video games, and he was a skilled bumper-car handler at the amusement park. But more importantly, he had observed his dad's outstanding automotive-vehicular control for years.

But now the time had come for him to try it for himself. He got behind the wheel. I lost the coin toss with my wife, so I got in the passenger seat. We strapped on our seat belts, and he easily maneuvered the car out of the driveway. I put on my best Obi-Wan Kenobi voice as I guided my young Padawan driver.

So far, so good. Signal light, apply gas pedal slowly, and off we go. Not bad for a rookie. He was looking confident and in control.

We headed out onto a country road and had clear sailing ahead of us. I thought it would be fun for him to experience the engine going into overdrive when the passing gear kicks in, just in case we needed to get ahead of a slower vehicle.[56]

I said, "On the count of three, step hard on the gas pedal for five seconds so you can feel the engine kick into passing gear."

He said, "Are you sure?"

"Yes," I scoffed. "Every driver needs to know what their car can do." This was going to be fun: the power, the speed, the exhilaration. My son was going to experience a little excitement on the road with his dad.

One…two…three…SCREEEEEEEEEEEEEECH!!!!!!!!

He stepped hard on the wrong pedal. After peeling my face off the glove compartment, I suggested that

---

56. Actually I just like driving fast. You should have seen me on the German autobahn!

perhaps I should drive if he was having trouble distinguishing between the only *two* pedals on the floor. So we spent some time with a few basics, such as adjusting the mirrors and practicing the signal lights.

It is one thing to watch others drive; it is quite another to get behind the wheel and do it yourself.

EXPERIENCING GOD

When it comes to a relationship with God, you can learn all about it from others if you want, but nothing compares to experiencing God for yourself. You can read every book out there about God and still not know Him personally. Like most things, that takes time and experience. This brings us to our last truth we want to share with you. This builds on all the others and helps you take that final step in knowing and doing the will of God.

Truth #7: You come to know God by experience as you obey Him and He accomplishes His work through you.

As we have mentioned several times throughout this book, there's a world of difference between knowing *about* God and knowing God. Most people don't need more knowledge; they need to know how to act on the knowledge they already have.

Jesus said there will be many who think they knew God, only to find out that they really didn't have a relationship with Him after all (Matthew 7:21–23). The reason people lose interest in church is because they are not experiencing God in their lives. They hear a lot of sermons and Bible studies about Him, but they do not have a personal relationship with Him.

Isn't it sad when couples who have been married for decades shockingly announce that they are getting a divorce? How could two people live in the same house for so many years yet have no relationship? It's because proximity alone cannot grow a relationship. Is it possible that you could have been in church your entire life and been reading your Bible—yet not be any closer to Jesus than you've ever been?

WHAT IT MEANS TO KNOW GOD

Jesus said, "This is eternal life: that they may know You, the only true God, and the One You have sent—Jesus Christ" (John 17:3). Knowing God is to be the ultimate goal of every Christian. If you know Him personally, He knows you and welcomes you into His Kingdom. Those who do not know God are not going to experience Him. They will not be led by His Spirit. They will not benefit from His blessings, protection, or guidance.

DAY BY DAY

George Mueller was a Christian who lived during the 1800s. God led him to begin a ministry to orphans in Bristol, England.

With few financial resources to support his growing orphanage, George trusted in God to provide the means for what He had called him to do.

One day, with three hundred orphans sitting at the breakfast table, George received some troubling news from the kitchen. There was no food.

George voiced a simple prayer, "God, we thank you for what you are going to give us to eat. Amen."

Within a minute there was a knock on the front door. It was a baker. He had awakened at 3:00 a.m. thinking of the orphans. He felt compelled to bake them some bread for that day and had delivered it to them.

Moments later there was another knock on the door. It was the milkman. His cart had broken down just outside the orphanage. It would take some time to repair and all the milk would go bad unless the orphanage took it.

"Faith does not operate in the realm of the possible. There is no glory for God in that which is humanly possible. Faith begins where man's power ends."
— George Mueller

*If you've never read Mueller's story it's a great example of God working through an ordinary man in extraordinary ways.

Knowing God is more than head knowledge; it includes intimate relationship, experience, and first-hand interaction. The more time you spend with someone, the better you will know them. If you were to see Henry Blackaby's current Bible, you might feel sorry for him. It looks so tattered and worn. Some pages are loose, and on some spots the cover is worn through the finish. This is not because he can't afford a new Bible. In fact, over the years he has owned numerous Bibles. But he keeps wearing them out. Each of his five adult children possesses one of his old Bibles, and they all look the same: *used.* They testify to how much time he spends with God. He wants to know God better and better every day. He has a desire to be in God's presence, a desire to hear when God speaks, and a desire to follow each and every instruction God gives him.

I (Tom) inherited Henry's name (his middle name is Thomas) and his worn out Bible, and he set a remarkable example for me to follow. But the choice of whether to know God is up to me. No one can do that for someone else.

The apostle Paul said in Philippians 3:10, "My goal is to know Him and the power of His resurrection and the fellowship of His sufferings, being conformed to His death." There are no shortcuts to knowing God. You can't just read a book about Him or watch a movie about Him—you have to spend quality time with Him in order to know Him.

The closer you walk with Jesus, the more recognizable His voice will become for you. As you obey what He tells you, it will change your world. Not only you, but countless others will be affected by your decision to follow Christ.

THOSE WHO EXPERIENCE GOD CHANGE THE WORLD

Here are a few examples from church history of men and women through whom God worked in powerful ways to impact the world.

William Carey (1761–1834) was an ordinary young man who had been an apprentice to a shoe repairman at age fourteen. William began to have a passion to know God and wanted to serve Him, so he taught himself Latin, Greek, Hebrew, Italian, Dutch, and French while working on shoes. He also became deeply concerned about sharing the gospel in foreign lands, to those who had never heard about Jesus. This led him to do something that was unthinkable in his day—he moved to India as a missionary! He used his gift for languages to translate the Bible into Bengali and Sanskrit and printed parts of the Bible in forty-four other languages and dialects. Carey is considered by many to be the father of modern missions. Because of his example, many missionaries have since followed his lead and have taken the gospel all around the world.

William Wilberforce (1759–1833) grew up wealthy, spoiled, self-centered, and arrogant. His ambition in life was to sleep in, play cards, party with his friends, and live a life of ease in the government. He was well on his way to achieving these goals when God got a hold of his life. A particular issue of his day grabbed his heart: slavery. He believed slavery to be an immoral blight to society, so he joined the movement for the abolition of the slave trade in England. This allegiance would cost him his reputation and his health. It took from 1789 to 1833 before the official abolition of slavery in the United Kingdom, and Wilberforce persisted to the end. In fact, he died within months of hearing the final bill had been passed in the British House of Commons. The efforts of Wilberforce and his colleagues led directly to the liberating of 800,000 slaves. Today, you can find a statue of Wilberforce where he is buried in Westminster Abbey in London.[57]

Amy Carmichael (1867–1951) was born in Ireland. Her father died when she was five years old, and as a young girl she suffered from a painful debilitating disease of the nerves. Sometimes she was required to stay in bed for weeks at a time. At age twenty she heard the famous missionary Hudson Taylor speak at a conference and was convinced that God was calling her to be a missionary. After some years of training, she ended up in India where she focused her efforts on helping young girls who were forced into temple prostitution. She developed a great love for these girls and established a sanctuary for more than one thousand children rescued from the temples. Amy not only spent fifty-five years as a missionary in India, but she wrote thirty-five books. Amy died where she served in India, and a simple bird bath has been placed over her grave with the Tamil word for *mother* inscribed on it, "Amma." Amy's obedience to God's will for her life impacted thousands of people around the world. Our obedience, just like hers, can change the world around us more than we could ever imagine.

---

57. You can see his story in the 2006 film *Amazing Grace*.

"I'LL DO IT LATER"

 I (Dan) don't have what you'd call a "driven" personality. My motto is: "Why put off until tomorrow what you can put off indefinitely?" Over the years I have tested my dad's patience many times with my token phrase: "I'll do it later." I thought I was getting by just fine with this approach to life until my second semester of college.

A gentle shake brought my Thursday morning to an unexpected early beginning. Wiping the sleep from my eyes, I looked up to see my mother standing over my bed. "Daniel, you need to print off your final exam schedule."

Giving an annoyed shrug I muttered, "Yeah, I know, I'll do it later," and I went back to sleep. The day went on, and late that night my dad approached me (for the umpteenth time). "Dan, do you have your exam schedule figured out yet?" Finally the nagging got to me, and I quickly printed off my schedule and went on to bed.

Friday morning came, and I was feeling good. Glancing at my exam schedule, I saw that my first exam was at 9:00 a.m. I grabbed some breakfast to go and headed out the door.

8:30: *Ah-ha! Thirty minutes early and the first student here. Might as well do a bit of last minute cramming.*

8:45: *Wow, my professor sure is going to be impressed with me! Still the only one here!*

8:50: *I'm starting to get lonely. Where is everyone?*

Honestly, is it so hard to show up to a test a little early?
Come on guys, learn to be responsible like me!

    8:55: *Okay . . . soooo . . . am I in the right classroom?*

    9:01: *I'm in huge trouble. . . .*

In absolute horror I pulled out the crumpled piece of paper with my exam outline messily scribbled on it:

ROST 2203 Final:

Classroom-U117

Time: 9 a.m.

Day: THURSDAY

The biggest consequence I had to face was not getting a big solid *F* in that class. Nor was it the wasted tuition money. Both of those seemed like a weekend in Disneyland compared to what I had to do next: tell my dad.

OBEDIENCE

Has God ever asked you to do something, but you had other plans? Disobedience to God is always costly. How many times have you followed your own schedule instead of God's? How many times have you trusted your own best thinking and disregarded the wisdom of the Bible? Living according to God's will requires obedience. Sometimes it sounds nice to be your own boss— no one telling you what to do, no one getting on your case for leaving things undone, no one cramping your style. But the longer you walk with God, the more you'll realize that our ways are not His ways (Isaiah 55:8), and His ways are always the best!

What would you say the difference is between reading a comic book, a fiction novel, and an autobiography? The comic book is considered light reading where there are more pictures than words. The creators of the comic book do not give many details about the characters, nor do they make efforts to give background information to the sketch. They just tell a short story or make you laugh by drawing a funny situation. The author of a novel describes situations, characters, places, and the times in which the story takes place. They offer lots of background and many details, but even when the story is based on actual incidents, there is a lot of fictional information, or made up from the imagination of the writer. The purpose of a novel is generally to entertain the reader. Some do an amazing job and can even impact how you think about some things. An autobiography is quite different. In this type of book you have a chance to hear from an eyewitness, someone who lived what they are writing about. They remember the sights, the smells, the feelings they had, and other details that can help you feel like you were right there with them. Autobiographies seek to draw you into the world of the author and help you understand them better and have an informed appreciation for the situations about which they are writing. The Bible is God's autobiography; it is God's story about Himself. He wants you to feel what He feels and see what He sees. He wants you to become close to Him as He reveals to you who He is and what He is like.

REMBRANDT'S THE RETURN OF THE PRODIGAL SON

The great Dutch painter Rembrandt (1606–1669) painted many biblical scenes, including two pieces depicting the parable of the prodigal son. These two paintings also somewhat reflected his own life. In his younger days, he painted *The Prodigal Son in the Tavern*, which was a self-portrait depicting he and his wife Saskia as the prodigal and a prostitute in a brothel. At that time, his life was spent on foolish living, in which he accumulated massive debt. He was eventually forced to sell his possessions in order to get out of debt. Near the end of his life, he painted another painting about this parable called *The Return of the Prodigal Son*. In this painting, the prodigal is shown on his knees before his gracious father. It is a completely different scene and reflects the heart of a man who experienced the emptiness of worldly living and longed to be home with the person who loved him most.

The Bible testifies that when people had a God-initiated encounter, there were common elements of the experience:

* Every experience with God served to deepen the person's relationship with God and improve their understanding of who God is.

* Every experience with God built on the previous experiences as God revealed His will and His ways to the person.

* Every experience with God challenged the faith of the person God was working with.

* Every experience revealed the person's complete dependence on God to complete the task.

* Every experience brought clear instructions from God that were easy to under—stand, but often took great courage to follow.

God wants to be active in your life just as He has been active in the lives of so many people throughout history. But you cannot experience God without spending time with Him. Many times we want to jump ahead in life without being ready. We want to run before we can crawl. Before you can ever obey God, you must first spend time with Him so you know what He wants you to obey. Key people throughout history have responded to God's invitation to join Him in what He wanted to do. Because they said yes to God, the world has never been the same. You have the same opportunity. Will you accept it?

WALKING WITH GOD

1. In your own words, summarize what it means to experience God at work in and through your life.

2. Is there a situation you are facing today in which you need God's intervention?

3. Is there something you are passionate about that God may want to use for His purposes?

4. Is there something specific you could do today to step out in obedience to what God is telling you?

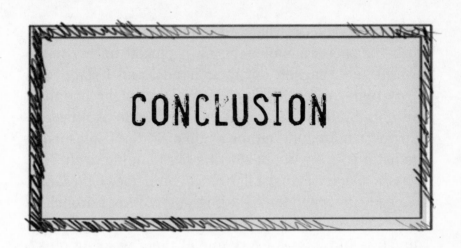

CONCLUSION

Not long ago I (Dan) was somehow talked into registering to run a half marathon by my little sister. The problem was that my sister had been faithfully jogging every day for the past four years. I, on the other hand, worked up a sweat just walking to the kitchen and back to grab my plate of nachos.

Digging out my old running clothes from the storage bin, I decided to take my body out for a test run and see what I had to work with. The answer? Not much! About half a mile into my jog, I felt like I had been hit by a bus. My entire body throbbed with pain, sweat poured off my forehead like Niagara Falls, and I was breathing like Darth Vader. That's when, through divine providence, I noticed a second trail that veered off back in the direction of my apartment. Wishing to end my misery, and hobbling like an old man, I slowly merged onto the new trail. . . .

And there was a deafening eruption of cheering! To my surprise there were suddenly large crowds of people lining both sides of the trail applauding and hollering words of encouragement to me. I picked up my pace. Several kids reached out their hands, and I slapped a hardy high-five as I galloped past, producing ooohhhs and ahhhhs from the captivated multitude. A little girl scurried out and offered me a cup of water. I splashed it against my face without slowing my blinding dash.

As a cloud of dust billowed behind me, I threaded the needle between the irritatingly slow, sweat-drenched joggers clogging up the trail. Why were there so many runners—and why is every one of them wearing pink? That's when I noticed the large pink banner beside the path: Avon Walk for Breast Cancer – Mile 32. I had just stumbled into the middle of a breast cancer awareness run!

Finishing a long race is a lot easier when you just skip straight to the end. Don't you sometimes wish life worked like that? We enjoy the cheering crowds and the feeling of accomplishment, but we aren't usually as eager to deal with the weaving road, the ups and downs, and the aches required to get there.

If there is only one thing you've gleaned from reading this book, we hope you understand that there is no quick, easy, one-size-fits-all formula for experiencing God's purposes in your life. In the race of life, there are no shortcuts. The seven steps in this book are merely a guide to get you to the right path and point you in the right direction—but you are the only one that can run the race.

With that in mind, allow us to recap the seven steps one more time.

Here we go. . . .

THE SEVEN STEPS

God is ALWAYS at work around you. Are you watching?

God pursues a LOVE relationship with you. Are you responding?

God invites you to JOIN HIM in what He is doing. Are you willing?

God will SPEAK to you through His Spirit. Are you listening?

God will bring you to a crisis of BELIEF. Are you going to pass the test?

You will have to make ADJUSTMENTS in your life. Are you prepared to do it?

You will EXPERIENCE God as you obey Him. Are you ready for the next adventure?

So now you know the Seven[58] Steps . . . Seven Realities, Seven Truths, Seven Principles, Seven Guidelines. It doesn't really matter what you call them, because the steps are not what is important—experiencing God in your life is. Having a growing, thriving, ever-deepening, meaningful relationship with Him is the goal, not taking seven steps in the right direction. The Christian life is not about a method or a program; it is about a person—Jesus Christ. As you walk with Him, He will lead you on many more steps that will take you on an incredible adventure.

YOUR FUTURE IS NOT YET WRITTEN

Your future has not yet been written, but God already knows what it could be if you choose to follow Him. Every choice you make has an impact on your future. From the moment you wake up, you are choosing whether or not to get out of bed or sleep a little longer. You choose what to wear, what to have for breakfast, whether to give yourself plenty of time or whether you will have to rush out the door. Who will you sit with on the bus or at lunch time? Will you listen to the teacher in class or doodle on your notebook? Will you sneak a few text messages in during class or not risk getting

---

58. Seven is a special number in the Bible being used about six hundred times. It signifies perfection, divine fullness, and completeness. The Hebrew word for *seven* means "to have enough, to be full, to be satisfied." Check out how many sevens there are in Joshua 6:1–20 alone. Revelation contains by far the most sevens: seven churches, seven seals, seven trumpets, seven personages, seven vials, seven woes, and seven new things. In Isaiah 11:2. the Holy Spirit rested on Jesus in seven distinct ways: Spirit of God, wisdom, understanding, counsel, power, knowledge, and fear of God.

your phone confiscated? Sometimes you may go through your entire day and not think about God even once. In fact, you may not even realize He has been pushed out of your mind by other priorities and interests.

Choosing to put God in the center of your life is the best decision you can ever make.

Here are some ways you can be intentional about growing in your faith:

* Make it a habit now to spend time reading His Word every day.

* Pray often.

* Make the most of opportunities to be in Bible study. Don't settle for those "Sunday school answers."

* Seek out wise Christians and spend time with them. Ask them questions. Listen to how they pray and observe how they interact with others. This is especially important if your parents are not Christians.

God has plans for your life, but it will be up to you whether or not you choose to walk down His pathways marked out for you, or whether you will make your own way through life.

Don't forget: The Christian life is not about what you want to do for God; it is what God wants to do through you. If through this book you have made a new commitment to Christ, have a deeper walk with God, and are better able to let the Spirit of God lead you, then we have succeeded. Our prayer is that God will have His way in your heart and that you will experience Him every day of your life from now on.

KEEP WALKING . . .

From Tom

I typically travel more than 75,000 miles by plane each year. When traveling I constantly ask questions to keep my focus on God and to look for clues for what He is up to around me. I wonder if I am sitting beside a person on the plane randomly or if it is a divine appointment that will change my life or theirs. During my wait times, I ask God if there is someone I need to be praying for or writing an encouraging e-mail. I ask questions of the person who picks me up at the airport wondering if I can partner with them in prayer over something in their life. All the time I am asking to clarify what He wants me to share with the people where I will be speaking next.

Then at the end of the day, I take a moment to reflect and see if there may have been something I missed or if there is someone I need to follow up with in the coming days. When you let God guide your mind and thoughts, you will be amazed at all the things He will direct your attention to. Always remember He is the Lord; we are the servants.

From Dan

You made it! Whatever your reasons for reading this book were, I pray that we helped in some small way to point you toward our amazing God who loves you. Making decisions about your life and future is a scary and overwhelming thing. I remember the uneasy feeling I had as high school graduation approached, and I still didn't know what God wanted me to do with my life. All my friends seemed to have a clear calling (to seminary, to college, to the workforce, to missions), but I didn't have a clue!

I decided to commit a full year to traveling, trying out different forms of ministry, and seeking God's will for my life. I went to South Africa (college ministry), Greece (refugee work), Brazil (medical missions), Germany (intercultural ministry), and Norway (youth ministry). By the end of that year, I knew God was calling me to pursue ministry full-time. Don't be discouraged if God takes you on a journey that looks different than those around you, but do whatever it takes until you feel God's peace about your calling.

If you're like me, you may be guilty of thinking that if we don't live according to God's plan, then God is the one who misses out on our irreplaceable service. I've learned otherwise. God never needed us to begin with! When we

> "I used to ask God to help me. Then I asked if I might help Him. I ended up by asking Him to do His work through me."
>
> —Hudson Taylor

fail to live according to God's plan, in the end we are the ones to miss out. It's never too late to come back to God, but I encourage you not to waste even a single day of your life living anything less than God's best!

From Mike

I sincerely hope you enjoyed our little journey together. I often think back to a time when I got stuck driving in The-Middle-of-Nowhere Virginia. I some-how ended up on some scary back roads going through a heavily wooded area. Then all sorts of stuff happened at once: my cell phone died, my car's gas warning light turned on, my GPS stopped working, the sun began setting, and I started seeing people with dogs and guns (not even joking). It was like the set-up of a horror movie! I just kept praying, "God, please help me come across a main highway, preferably with a gas station and no serial killer cannibal hillbillies."

Obviously, I made it out alive (except for the emotional scars, that is). That's just one of many experiences that has taught me the importance of knowing where you are going. The time to cry out to God is not after you've taken many wrong turns and are in a place of desperation. Develop a personal relationship with God now, and you'll have a lifetime of walking with Him as He reveals His will for you.

When I was eighteen, I felt God clearly calling me to be a pastor. It scared me to death! I wanted to do anything but stand up in front of people and preach! But I took that step, and man I'm glad I did. God has taken me places already in my life I had never dreamed possible. What does God have in store for you? What is God's will for your life? Only time will tell as you experience Him and He guides you. I'll leave you the advice I often give those in my own ministry: keep moving forward. This book is about steps. You don't have to be going at the same pace as everybody else, but you do need to keep moving forward. Don't get caught standing still in life! Walk by faith step-by-step, and there is no telling where God might take you.

P.S. When Henry Blackaby preaches, he often holds up his tattered Bible (it's so soft, it bends in half) and makes this statement to the audience: "Don't take my word for it. Read it in here!"

There is no better way we can think of to leave you than to say the same thing to you. We have done our prayerful best to be faithful to the Scriptures in this book. But don't take our word for it. Grab a Bible and check it out for yourself.

ABOUT THE AUTHORS

Mike Blackaby is the oldest son of Richard and Lisa and the oldest grandson of Henry Blackaby. He is currently working on his PhD in Worldview and Apologetics from Southern Baptist Theological Seminary. Mike has been the minister to college and young adults at First Baptist Church in Jonesboro, Georgia, since 2010. He grew up in Canada where he enjoyed hockey and snowboarding, and played drums and guitar in several bands. He is a huge fan of Star Wars, rock 'n' roll, and Chinese food, but hates spiders and waiting in long lines. In 2011, he coauthored his first book, *When Worlds Collide: Stepping Up and Standing Out in an Anti-God Culture*, with his brother Daniel.

Daniel Blackaby is a fourth generation author. He grew up in Canada where he met and married his beautiful wife Sarah. He is a graduate of Golden Gate Baptist Theological Seminary with an MDiv. He has had several books published, including *When Worlds Collide: Stepping Up and Standing Out in an Anti-God Culture* and the fantasy fiction trilogy The Lost City Chronicles. He is a passionate advocate for a Christian "reclaiming" of the Arts. Daniel also loves classic literature, playing guitar, hockey (Go Sabres!) and baseball (Go Giants!). Follow his journey and writings at www. danielblackaby.com.

 *Tom Blackaby* is the second son of best-selling author Dr. Henry Blackaby (*Experiencing God: Knowing and Doing the Will of God*). He holds a BEd, MDiv and DMin. Tom has served as associate pastor of music/youth/education in four churches and served seven years as senior pastor of North Sea Baptist Church in Stavanger, Norway. Currently he is the International Director for Blackaby Ministries International and leads confer-ences/seminars speaking around the world. Tom loves to travel (forty countries so far!) and somehow found the time to author or coauthor these books:

The Man God Uses (and *The Student God Uses* version)

Anointed to Be God's Servants: Lessons from the Life of Paul and His Companions

The Blackaby Study Bible

Encounters with God Daily Bible

The Family God Uses

Experiencing God's Love in the Church

The Commands of Christ

Sammy Experiences God (children's book)

Experiencing God at Home

Experiencing God at Home Family Devotional

Tom and Kim have three kids and currently live near Vancouver, Canada, where they actively serve in their local church.

NOTES